Two-Color Quilts

Ten Romantic Red Quilts

from Nancy J. Martin

Martingale

& C O M P A N Y

Bothell, Washington

ACKNOWLEDGMENTS

Special thanks are extended to:

Cleo Nollette, who helped cut, stitch, and illustrate the quilts;

Virginia Lauth and Peggy Hinchey, for providing quilts;

Amanda Miller's fine quilters: Mabel Beechy, Mrs. Ida Miller, Alma Miller, Emma Raber, Celesta Schlabach, Mrs. Henry Schlabach, Mrs. Emma Shetler, Mrs. Sam Swartzentruber, Mrs. Jr. E. Troyer, Betty Weaver, and Katie Yoder;

Alvina Nelson and Hazel Montague, for their fine hand quilting;

Roxanne Carter, for machine quilting;

Pam Klopfer, for computer entry;

Dan Martin, for computer support.

CREDITS

Editor-in-Chief . . . . Kerry I. Smith
Technical Editors . . . . Christine Barnes
                                              Ursula Reikes
Managing Editor . . . . Judy Petry
Design Director . . . . Cheryl Stevenson
Cover Designer . . . . Jim Gerlitz
Text Designer . . . . Laurel Strand
Production Assistant . . . . Marijane E. Figg
Copy Editor . . . . Liz McGehee
Illustrator . . . . Laurel Strand
Photographer . . . . Brent Kane

MISSION STATEMENT

We are dedicated to providing quality products and service by working together to inspire creativity and to enrich the lives we touch.

Two-Color Quilts:
Ten Romantic Red Quilts from Nancy J. Martin
© 1998 by Nancy J. Martin

Martingale & Company
PO Box 118
Bothell, WA 98041-0118 USA

Printed in Hong Kong
03 02 01 00 99 98   6 5 4 3 2 1

Library of Congress Cataloging-in-Publication Data

Martin, Nancy J.
    Two-color quilts : ten romantic red quilts from
        Nancy J. Martin.
        p. cm.
    ISBN 1-56477-217-9
    1. Patchwork — Patterns. 2. Quilting— Patterns.
3. Appliqué — Patterns. 4. Color in textile crafts. I. Title.
TT835.M2735 1998
746.45'041—dc21   97-46891
                                                  CIP

Contents

Preface

Two-color quilts have been a favorite of traditional quilters for more than one hundred fifty years. The high contrast in a two-color quilt, especially one stitched in red or blue against a crisp white background, creates a strong graphic appeal. Long admired by quilt collectors, these quilts work in both country and contemporary decorating schemes.

Why were many early quilts stitched in red and white or indigo and white fabrics? Patricia Mainardi, author of *Quilts: The Great American Art,* attributes the predominance of these color schemes to the permanence of the dyes: "Even in their choice of material, women quiltmakers behaved similarly to other artists. They wanted to use only the most permanent materials, and the popularity of two colors, indigo and turkey red (an alizarin dye), was the result of their ability to withstand much use without fading."[1]

The choice of white as a background was probably an economic one. Large amounts of fabric were needed for the background, and undyed cotton was less expensive than calico.[2]

The red-and-white color scheme became popular in the 1840s for a number of reasons: personal taste, the availability of fabrics, and the colorfastness of turkey red cotton. According to Barbara Brackman, author of *Clues in the Calico,* "Both plain and printed fabrics dyed with turkey red became a staple in clothing and quilts during the second quarter of the nineteenth century and lasted until the end."[3]

Blue and white was favored for woven coverlets, which became popular before the 1840s.[4] This color combination was both inexpensive and practical because indigo blue was a widely available and colorfast dye that would not run onto white. Around 1840, blue and white also became a popular color scheme for pieced and appliqué quilts.[5] Women of the period knew that indigo dye would be equally reliable on cotton prints, inspiring them to adapt this color scheme for their quilts.

According to Rod Kiracofe and Mary Elizabeth Johnson, authors of *The American Quilt,* ". . . in the last half of the nineteenth century, the one-color combination that surpassed all others in popularity was indigo blue and white. In a quiltmaker's body of work, there nearly always was at least one blue-and-white quilt. Often, she saved for her blue-and-white her fanciest quilting, sometimes making elaborate stuffed-work designs. . . . By the mid-19th century, women were well aware of the superiority of indigo as a dye. Textile mills responded by printing thousands of indigo blue-and-white designs, and many were offered through mail-order catalogues."[6]

Some quilt historians have recently theorized that the popularity of the blue-and-white color combination was a result of the influence of the Women's Christian Temperance Union (WCTU). This organization, dedicated to publicizing alcohol's threat to the family, was founded in Ohio and had as its colors blue and white. Many fine blue-and-white quilts, some done in the Drunkard's Path pattern, have been found in this area. However, there is little evidence to substantiate this theory.[7]

It is more likely that women of this era preferred this pleasant color scheme. In an 1898 issue of *The Modern Priscilla* magazine, an article states, "Color harmony is the key-note to success [in patchwork], and simplicity the next most important consideration. . . . All things considered, [a] pretty indigo blue and white print and white muslin combine beauty with the coveted old-time air more effectively than any style of cotton patchwork."[8]

1. Patricia Mainardi, *Quilts: The Great American Art* (Pedro, Calif.: Miles & Weir, Ltd., 1978), p. 6.
2. Elizabeth V. Warren and Sharon L. Eisenstat, *Glorious American Quilts* (New York: Penguin Books, 1996), p. 38.
3. Barbara Brackman, *Clues in the Calico* (McLean, Va.: EPM Publications, Inc., 1989), p. 63.
4. Warren and Eisenstat, *Glorious American Quilts*, p. 54.
5. Barbara Brackman, "Blue-and-White Quilts," *Quilter's Newsletter Magazine*, March 1987, p. 23.
6. Roderick Kiracofe and Mary Elizabeth Johnson, *The American Quilt* (New York: Clarkson N. Potter, 1993), p. 127.
7. Ibid., p. 128.
8. Katherine B. Johnson, "New Ideas In Patchwork," *The Modern Priscilla*, May 1898, p. 7.

Introduction

The appeal of red-and-white or blue-and-white quilts remains strong with quilters of today. As I travel and teach, many of my students tell me that they enjoy hand quilting more than piecing. Thus, they look for fast-and-easy block designs with lots of white space on which they can lavish hand quilting. I've provided directions for several quilts that fill this need.

Although this book is entitled *Two-Color Quilts*, the quilts are not necessarily two-fabric quilts. Many are scrappy, using either a variety of red prints or blue prints. The background colors vary from pure white to ecru to beige. This variation provides even more visual interest and depth in the designs.

To add to the fun of this project, *Two-Color Quilts* has been published as a topsy-turvy book. Following the instructions for the ten Romantic Red Quilts is basic information on all aspects of quiltmaking. Turn the book over, and you will find instructions for ten True-Blue Quilts.

Two-Color Quilts has been an enjoyable project, both in researching and stitching the quilts. I hope you find similar pleasure as you work with these time-honored, traditional designs.

Nancy J. Martin

About the Author

Nancy J. Martin, talented author, teacher, and quiltmaker, has written more than twenty-five books on quiltmaking. Nancy is an innovator in the quilting industry and introduced the Bias Square® cutting ruler to quilters everywhere. Along with more than twenty years of teaching experience and numerous classic quilting titles to her credit, Nancy is the founder and president of Martingale & Company, the publisher of America's Best-Loved Quilt Books®. Nancy and her husband, Dan, enjoy living in the Pacific Northwest.

Using This Book

This book contains complete instructions for twenty rotary-cut quilts: ten Romantic Red ones and ten True-Blue ones. The red quilts start on the next page; flip the book over to find the beginning of the blue quilts. Basic quiltmaking information can be found in the middle between the red and blue sections.

All the patterns are written for rotary cutting; a few quilts require appliqué or placement templates.

All measurements include ¼"-wide seam allowances. Read the complete cutting and piecing directions for the quilt you want to make before you begin. The patterns are graded as to difficulty, so match the pattern to your skill and patience level.

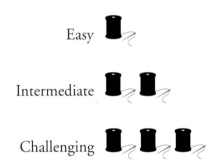

Easy

Intermediate

Challenging

The "Materials" section of each pattern includes fabric and color suggestions. Fabric requirements are based on 44"-wide fabric that has 42 usable inches after washing. If, after preshrinking, your fabric is not at least 42" wide, you may need to purchase more.

Cut strips across the fabric width, selvage to selvage, unless otherwise noted. Cutting specifications are given for strips that are 42" long when cut across the fabric width. If preshrunk fabric is less than 42", you may need to cut an additional strip to cut the required number of pieces.

Many of the quilts specify the purchase of fat quarters and fat eighths. Fat quarters should be 18" x 22", and fat eighths should be 9" x 22". Measure them to make sure. You may need to purchase additional fabric if your pieces are smaller than these measurements. If your fabric doesn't yield enough bias squares, substitute scraps of a look-alike fabric. Directions for making small amounts of bias squares are on page 59.

Always cut the largest pieces first from fat quarters or fat eighths, before cutting the smaller pieces. To achieve a scrappy look, purchase a variety of fat quarters or fat eighths. You will not always use all the fabric, so save leftovers for your next scrappy quilt.

Cutting instructions are geared for rotary cutting. Quick-cutting and strip-piecing techniques sometimes yield more pieces than are needed to make a particular block or quilt. Don't worry if you have a few more pieces than you need; save them for another scrap project.

All measurements include ¼"-wide seam allowances. *Do not add seam allowances to the dimensions given in the cutting section.* Cutting specifications for triangles indicate the size of the square from which you will cut the triangles. Directions for half-square triangles instruct you to "cut once diagonally"; instructions for quarter-square triangles specify "cut twice diagonally." If you need a refresher, see pages 53–54.

Use the photos and drawings that accompany the patterns as a reference while assembling your quilt. General instructions for finishing your quilt begin on page 66.

Most of the quilts have borders with straight-cut corners rather than mitered corners. You can cut border strips along the crosswise grain and seam them to get the length needed. Unless lengthwise borders are included in a quilt plan's fabric requirements, purchase additional fabric if you want to cut borders along the lengthwise grain. *Cut border pieces longer than the dimensions given, then trim them to fit when you know the actual dimensions of the center of the quilt top.* (See "Adding Borders" on page 66.) Bindings are made from narrow double-fold bias strips. (See "Binding the Edges" on pages 72–73.)

Romantic Red Quilts

Hovering Hawks

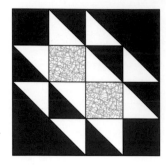

Hovering Hawks

DIMENSIONS: 48" x 48"
FINISHED BLOCK SIZE: 8" x 8"

16 blocks, stitched in reverse colorations, set 4 across and 4 down; 2"-wide inner border, 2"-wide Sawtooth border, and 4"-wide outer Sawtooth border.

MATERIALS: 44"-WIDE FABRIC

10 fat quarters of light-background red prints
10 fat quarters of dark-background red prints
8 small scraps (5" x 5") of medium-background red prints
⅜ yd. light-background print for inner border
3 yds. fabric for backing
½ yd. fabric for 200" (5½ yds.) of bias binding

CUTTING
ALL MEASUREMENTS INCLUDE ¼"-WIDE SEAMS.

From EACH fat quarter of light-background red print, cut:
2 squares, each 8" x 8", for bias squares. Cut an extra 8" square from one of the prints for a total of 21 squares.
3 squares (30 total), each 4⅞" x 4⅞". Cut once diagonally to make 60 large triangles for blocks and outer Sawtooth border. You will use 56 and have 4 left over.
2 squares (20 total), each 2½" x 2½", for blocks and inner Sawtooth border.
2 squares (20 total), each 2⅞" x 2⅞". Cut once diagonally to make 40 small triangles for blocks. You will use 32 and have 8 left over.

From the remaining light-background prints, cut:
4 squares, each 4½" x 4½", for corners of outer Sawtooth border.

From EACH fat quarter of dark-background red print, cut:
2 squares, each 8" x 8", for bias squares. Cut an extra 8" square from one of the prints for a total of 21 squares. Pair each dark-background square with an 8" light-background square, right sides up. Cut and piece 2½"-wide bias strips, following the directions for bias squares on pages 57–59. Cut 168 bias squares, each 2½" x 2½".
3 squares (30 total), each 4⅞" x 4⅞". Cut once diagonally to make 60 large triangles for blocks and outer Sawtooth border. You will use 56 and have 4 left over.
2 squares (20 total), each 2½" x 2½", for blocks. You will use 16 and have 4 left over.
2 squares (20 total), each 2⅞" x 2⅞". Cut once diagonally to make 40 small triangles for blocks. You will use 32 and have 8 left over.

From EACH small scrap of medium-background red print, cut:
4 squares (32 total), each 2" x 2".

From the light-background print for inner border, cut:
4 strips, each 2½" x 42".

DIRECTIONS

1. For the 8 light-background blocks, divide the bias squares and other pieces so the light and dark fabrics for each block match. You will need:
   6 bias squares
   2 large light triangles
   2 small light squares
   2 medium-background print squares
   4 small dark triangles that match the bias squares

HOVERING HAWKS, pieced by Nancy J. Martin, 1997, Woodinville, Washington, 48" x 48".
Blocks stitched in reverse light-and-dark colorations and turned in opposite directions form a pattern
reminiscent of Ocean Waves. Small and large Sawtooth borders surround the blocks. Quilted by Betty Weaver.

2. For the 8 dark-background blocks, divide the bias squares and other pieces in the same manner. You will need:
   6 bias squares
   2 large dark triangles
   2 small dark squares
   2 medium-background print squares
   4 small light triangles that match the bias squares

3. To make a light-background block, join the bias squares, small dark triangles, small light squares, and medium squares into rows. Join the rows.

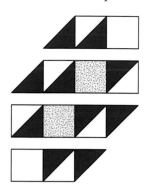
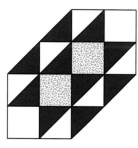

Make 8.

4. Add 2 large light triangles to complete 1 light-background Hovering Hawks block. Make 8 blocks.

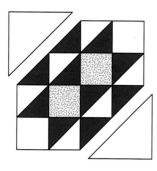
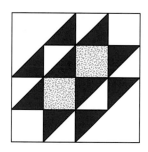

Make 8.

5. Repeat with the remaining pieces to make 8 dark-background blocks.

Make 8.

6. Join 2 light- and 2 dark-background blocks as shown for Row A. Make 2 of Row A. Join the remaining light- and dark-background blocks as shown to make 2 of Row B.

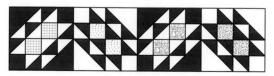

Row A
Make 2.

Row B
Make 2.

7. Join Rows A and B, alternating the rows.

8. Add the 2½"-wide inner border strips, following the directions for borders on pages 66–67.

9. Join 18 bias squares, each 2½" x 2½", with 9 facing in each direction, to make 1 Sawtooth border. Make 4 borders. Add a 2½" light-background square to each end of 2 of the borders.

Make 2.

Make 2.

10. Add the shorter border strips to the sides of the quilt top. Add the longer border strips to the top and bottom of the quilt top.

11. Join a large light and a large dark triangle. Make 40 units.

Make 40.

12. Join 10 units made in Step 11, with 5 facing in each direction, to make 1 Sawtooth border. Make 4 borders. Add a 4½" light-background square to each end of 2 of the borders.

Make 2.

Make 2.

13. Add the shorter border strips to the sides of the quilt top. Add the longer border strips to the top and bottom of the quilt top.
14. Layer the quilt top with batting and backing. Quilt or tie. See the quilting suggestion at right.
15. Bind the edges with the bias strips.

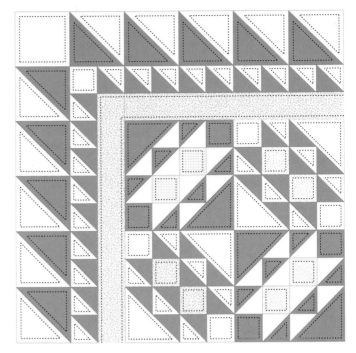

Double Nine Patch

Double Nine Patch

DIMENSIONS: 49⅛" X 62"
FINISHED BLOCK SIZE: 9" X 9"

12 blocks, set diagonally 3 across and 4 down; 5½"-wide border.

MATERIALS: 44"-WIDE FABRIC

3 yds. white tone-on-tone fabric for blocks, setting triangles, and border
¾ yd. red fabric for Nine Patch blocks
3⅛ yds. fabric for backing (crosswise join)
½ yd. fabric for 230" (6½ yds.) of bias binding

CUTTING
ALL MEASUREMENTS INCLUDE ¼"-WIDE SEAMS.

From the white tone-on-tone fabric, cut:
11 strips, each 1½" x 42", for Nine Patch blocks.
2 strips, each 5¾" x 51½", along the lengthwise grain, for side borders.
2 strips, each 5¾" x 49⅛", along the lengthwise grain, for top and bottom borders.
6 squares, each 9½" x 9½", for alternate blocks.
3 squares, each 14" x 14". Cut twice diagonally to make 12 side setting triangles. You will use 10 and have 2 left over.
2 squares, each 7¼" x 7¼". Cut once diagonally to make 4 corner setting triangles.
48 squares, each 3½" x 3½", for Nine Patch blocks.

From the red fabric, cut:
13 strips, each 1½" x 42", for Nine Patch blocks.

DIRECTIONS

NOTE
The following instructions are for the traditional nine-patch construction method. For an alternative method, see pages 55–56.

1. Join two 1½"-wide red strips and a 1½"-wide white strip to make Strip Set 1. Press the seams toward the red fabric. The strip set should measure 3½" wide when sewn. Make 5 strip sets. Crosscut the strip sets into 120 segments, each 1½" wide.

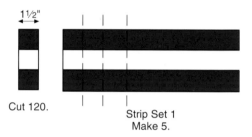

Cut 120.

Strip Set 1
Make 5.

2. Join two 1½"-wide white strips and a 1½"-wide red strip to make Strip Set 2. Press the seams toward the red fabric. The strip set should measure 3½" wide when sewn. Make 3 strip sets. Crosscut the strip sets into 60 segments, each 1½" wide.

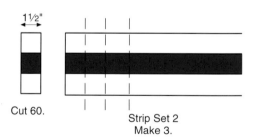

Cut 60.

Strip Set 2
Make 3.

3. Join the segments as shown to make 1 nine-patch unit. Make 60 nine-patch units.

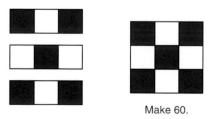

Make 60.

DOUBLE NINE PATCH, pieced by Cleo Nollette, 1997, Seattle, Washington, 49⅛" x 62".
This simple strip-pieced, two-fabric quilt makes a great beginner project.
Quilted by Mrs. Emma Shetler.

4. Join 5 nine-patch units and 4 white 3½" squares into rows; join the rows to make 1 Double Nine Patch block. Make 12 blocks.

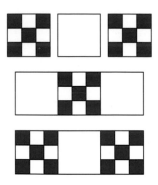  

Make 12.

5. Stitch Nine Patch blocks, alternate blocks, and side setting triangles into diagonal rows. Join the rows. Add the corner setting triangles.

6. Add the 5¾" x 51½" border strips to the sides of the quilt top, following the instructions for borders on pages 66–67. Add the 5¾" x 49⅛" border strips to the top and bottom of the quilt top.

7. Layer the quilt top with batting and backing. Tie or quilt. See the quilting suggestion below.

8. Bind the edges with the bias strips.

Double X

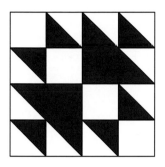

Double X

DIMENSIONS: 66" X 98"
FINISHED BLOCK SIZE: 8" X 8"

23 blocks, set with 22 alternate plain blocks, 5 across and 9 down; 2"-wide inner border; 4"-wide Flying Geese border with pieced corner squares; 7"-wide outer border.

MATERIALS: 44"-WIDE FABRIC

7½ yds. white fabric for blocks, inner border, and outer border
2⅜ yds. red fabric for blocks and pieced border
5¾ yds. fabric for backing (lengthwise join)
⅝ yd. fabric for 338" (9⅜ yds.) of bias binding

CUTTING
ALL MEASUREMENTS INCLUDE ¼"-WIDE SEAMS.

From the white fabric, cut:
22 squares, each 8½" x 8½", for alternate blocks.
3 fat quarters, each 18" x 22", for bias squares.
2 strips, each 2½" x 72½", along the lengthwise grain, for side inner borders.
2 strips, each 2½" x 44½", along the lengthwise grain, for top and bottom inner borders.
2 strips, each 7¼" x 84½", along the lengthwise grain, for side outer borders.
2 strips, each 7¼" x 66", along the lengthwise grain, for top and bottom outer borders.
46 squares, each 2⅞" x 2⅞". Cut once diagonally to make 92 small triangles for blocks.
92 squares, each 2½" x 2½", for blocks.
128 squares, each 2⅞" x 2⅞". Cut once diagonally to make 256 small triangles for Flying Geese border and corner squares.

From the red fabric, cut:
23 squares, each 4⅞" x 4⅞". Cut diagonally to make 46 large triangles for blocks.
3 fat quarters, each 18" x 22". Pair each red fat quarter with a white fat quarter, right sides up. Cut and piece 2½"-wide bias strips, following the directions for bias squares on pages 57–59. Cut 138 bias squares, each 2½" x 2½".
30 squares, each 5¼" x 5¼". Cut twice diagonally to make 120 small triangles for Flying Geese border.
4 squares, each 3⅜" x 3⅜", for border corner squares.

DIRECTIONS

1. Join a 2½" white square and a bias square. Make an additional unit. Join the units as shown. Make 46.

Make 46.

2. Join a bias square and 2 small white triangles. Join this unit to a large red triangle. Make 46.

Make 46.

3. Join the units make in Steps 1 and 2. Make 46.

Make 46.

4. Join 2 of the units made in Step 3 to make 1 Double X block. Make 23 blocks.

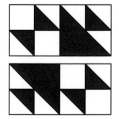

Make 23.

5. Join 3 Double X blocks and 2 alternate plain blocks to make 1 row. Make 5 rows.

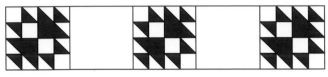

Make 5.

6. Join 3 alternate plain blocks and 2 Double X blocks to make 1 row. Make 4 rows.

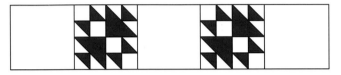

Make 4.

7. Join the rows, beginning and ending with a row that has 3 Double X blocks.

8. Join 2 small white triangles and a small red triangle to make 1 Flying Geese unit. Make 120 units.

Make 120.

9. Join 4 small white triangles and a red 3⅜" square to make 1 corner-square unit. Make 4 corner-square units.

Make 4.

10. Add the 2½" x 72½" inner border strips to the sides of the quilt top, following the directions for borders on pages 66–67. Add the 2½" x 44½" inner border strips to the top and bottom of the quilt top.

11. Join 38 Flying Geese units to make a side border. Make an additional side border. Add the borders to the quilt top.

12. Join 22 Flying Geese units to make the top border. Make an additional border for the bottom. Add a corner-square unit to each end of the top and bottom borders. Add the borders to the quilt top.

13. Add the 7¼" x 84½" outer border strips to the sides of the quilt top. Add the 7¼" x 66" outer border strips to the top and bottom of the quilt top.

14. Layer the quilt top with batting and backing. Quilt or tie. See the quilting suggestion below.

15. Bind the edges with the bias strips.

DOUBLE X, by Virginia Lauth, 1997, Seattle, Washington, 66" x 98".
A Flying Geese border accentuates the contrast in this striking but simple two-fabric quilt.

Georgetown Circle

Georgetown Circle

DIMENSIONS: 60" x 74"
FINISHED BLOCK SIZE: 12" x 12"

12 blocks, set 3 across and 4 down, with 2"-wide sashing and 8"-wide border.

MATERIALS: 44"-WIDE FABRIC

7 fat quarters of assorted dark-background red fabrics
6 fat quarters of assorted light-background red fabrics
6 fat quarters of assorted medium-background red fabrics
1⅞ yds. red print for border
3¾ yds. fabric for backing (crosswise join)
⅝ yd. fabric for 276" (7⅔ yds.) of bias binding

NOTE
Directions are for six pairs of identical blocks, which is the most economical way to purchase and use the fabric. If you have a large collection of scraps, don't hesitate to add red fabrics for a scrappier look, as shown in the photo.

CUTTING
ALL MEASUREMENTS INCLUDE ¼"-WIDE SEAMS.

From the assorted dark-background red fabrics, cut a total of:
6 squares, each 8" x 8", for bias squares.
6 squares, each 10" x 10", for bias squares.
31 strips, each 2½" x 12½", for sashing.

From the assorted light-background red fabrics, cut a total of:
6 squares, each 8" x 8". Pair each light-background square with an 8" dark-background square, right sides up. Cut and piece 2½"-wide bias strips, following the directions for bias squares on pages 57–59. Cut 48 bias squares, each 2⅝" x 2⅝".

From the assorted medium-background red fabrics, cut:
6 squares, each 10" x 10". Pair each square with a 10" dark-background square, right sides up. Cut and piece 3½"-wide bias strips. Cut 48 bias squares, each 3⅞" x 3⅞". Cut the bias squares once diagonally to make 96 half bias squares.

From EACH of the remaining light-background red fabrics, cut:
2 squares (12 total), each 4¾" x 4¾", for block center.
8 squares (48 total), each 3½" x 3½", for block corners.
4 squares (24 total), each 4¼" x 4¼". Cut twice diagonally to make 96 triangles for background.

From EACH of the remaining medium-background fabrics, cut:
4 squares (24 total), each 2½" x 2½", for sashing squares. You will use 20 and have 4 left over.
4 squares (24 total), each 3⅞" x 3⅞". Cut once diagonally to make 48 triangles to surround the center squares.

From the red print for the border, cut:
2 strips, each 8¼" x 58½", along the lengthwise grain, for side borders.
2 strips, each 8¼" x 60", along the lengthwise grain, for top and bottom borders.

GEORGETOWN CIRCLE, pieced by Cleo Nollette, 1997, Seattle, Washington, 60" x 74".
A long-standing collection of harmonious red scraps was the inspiration for this spirited star quilt.
Using a different fabric for each sashing strip and sashing square enhances the scrappy effect.
Quilted by Mrs. Ida Miller.

DIRECTIONS

1. Join 1 bias square, 2 light triangles, and 2 half bias squares as shown to make a unit. Make 4 units.

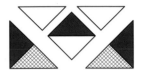

Make 4.

2. Join a 3½" light square to each end of 2 of the units made in Step 1.

3. Join 4 medium triangles to 1 light 4¾" square to make the center unit.

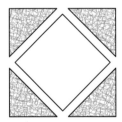

4. Join the remaining units made in Step 1 to the center unit.

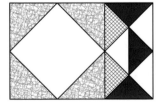

5. Join the units made in Steps 2 and 4 to make 1 Georgetown Circle block. Make 12 blocks.

Make 12.

6. Join 3 blocks and 4 sashing strips to make a row. Make 4 rows.

7. Join 4 sashing squares and 3 sashing strips to make a sashing row. Make 5 sashing rows.

8. Join the rows, alternating block and sashing rows.

9. Add the 8¼" x 58½" borders to the sides of the quilt top, following the directions for borders on pages 66–67. Add the 8¼" x 60" borders to the top and bottom of the quilt top.

10. Layer the quilt top with batting and backing. Quilt or tie. See the quilting suggestion below.

11. Bind the edges with the bias strips.

Be My Valentine

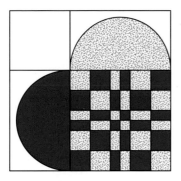

Woven Heart

DIMENSIONS: 73" X 73"
FINISHED BLOCK SIZE: 12" X 12"

9 blocks, set diagonally with alternate blocks and side and corner setting triangles; inner border of varying widths; 4½"-wide pieced ribbon border; 5"-wide outer border.

MATERIALS: 44"-WIDE FABRIC

3¼ yds. light-background print for blocks, setting triangles, and pieced ribbon border
4 fat quarters of dark red prints for hearts
4 fat quarters of contrasting red prints for hearts
1 fat eighth of dark red print for hearts
1 fat eighth of contrasting red print for hearts
2⅜ yds. dark red fabric for ribbon border and outer border
¼ yd. checked fabric for ribbon border
4½ yds. fabric for backing
⅝ yd. fabric for 300" (8⅓ yds.) of bias binding

CUTTING
ALL MEASUREMENTS INCLUDE ¼"-WIDE SEAMS.

From the light-background print, cut:
4 squares, each 12½" x 12½", for alternate blocks.
2 squares, each 18¼" x 18¼". Cut twice diagonally to make 8 side setting triangles.
2 squares, each 9½" x 9½". Cut once diagonally to make 4 corner setting triangles.
3 strips, each 2" x 42", for side inner borders.

2 strips, each 3½" x 42", for bottom inner border.
1 fat quarter, 18" x 22", for bias squares.
9 squares, each 5" x 5", for blocks.
18 rectangles, each 5" x 8", for blocks.
9 squares, each 7" x 7". Cut twice diagonally to make 36 large triangles for ribbon border.
10 squares, each 4⅛" x 4⅛". Cut twice diagonally to make 40 small triangles for ribbon border.
2 squares, each 6¾" x 6¾". Cut once diagonally to make 4 corner triangles for ribbon border.

From EACH dark and contrasting fat quarter of red prints, cut:
2 heart pieces (16 total) for appliqué, using the heart-top template on page 25.
2 strips (16 total), each 2" x 22", for blocks.
1 strip (8 total), 1¼" x 22", for blocks.

From EACH dark and contrasting fat eighth of red prints, cut:
1 heart piece (2 total) for appliqué, using the heart-top template on page 25.
2 strips (4 total), each 2" x 12", for blocks.
1 strip (2 total), 1¼" x 12", for blocks.

From the dark red fabric for the ribbon border and outer border, cut:
2 strips, each 5¼" x 63½", along the lengthwise grain, for outer side borders.
2 strips, each 5¼" x 73", along the lengthwise grain, for outer top and bottom borders.
1 fat quarter, 18" x 22", for bias squares. Pair the fat quarter with the light-background fat quarter, right sides up. Cut and piece 2½"-wide bias strips, following the directions for bias squares on pages 57–59. Cut 40 bias squares, each 2½" x 2½", for ribbon border.
9 squares, each 4⅛" x 4⅛". Cut twice diagonally to make 36 small triangles for ribbon border.
40 squares, each 2½" x 2½", for ribbon border.

From the checked fabric, cut:
40 squares, each 2½" x 2½", for ribbon border.

DIRECTIONS

1. Join the 2" x 22" and 1¼" x 22" dark and contrasting red print strips as shown to make a strip set. Repeat with the 2" x 12" and 1¼" x 12" dark and contrasting red print strips to make an additional strip set, for a total of 9 strip sets. The strip sets should measure 8" wide when sewn. Crosscut the strip sets into the segments shown. Cut segments for 2 hearts from each fat-quarter combination, and segments for 1 heart from the fat-eighth combination.

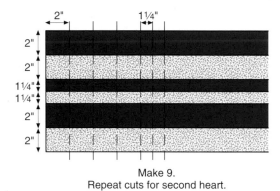

Make 9.
Repeat cuts for second heart.

2. Join the segments to form the woven section of each heart.

3. Appliqué a dark heart piece to a 5" x 8" light-background rectangle, following the directions for appliqué on pages 64–65. Repeat with a contrasting heart piece on another rectangle.

4. Join the woven section, appliquéd rectangles, and a 5" light-background square to make 1 Woven Heart block. Make 9 blocks.

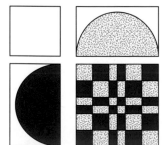

Make 9.

5. Join the Woven Heart blocks, alternate blocks, and side setting triangles into diagonal rows. Join the rows. Add the corner setting triangles.

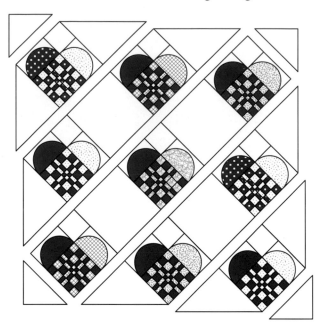

6. Piece the 2"-wide light-background strips and add them to the sides of the quilt top, following the directions for borders on pages 66–67. Piece and add the 3½"-wide light-background strip to the bottom of the quilt top. The quilt top should measure 54½" x 54½"; if not, adjust the inner borders to the correct size.

7. Join bias squares, squares, and triangles as shown to make 2 ribbon borders for the top and bottom of the quilt.

Make 1.   Make 8.   Make 1.

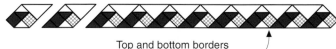

Top and bottom borders
Make 2.
Sew this edge to quilt top.

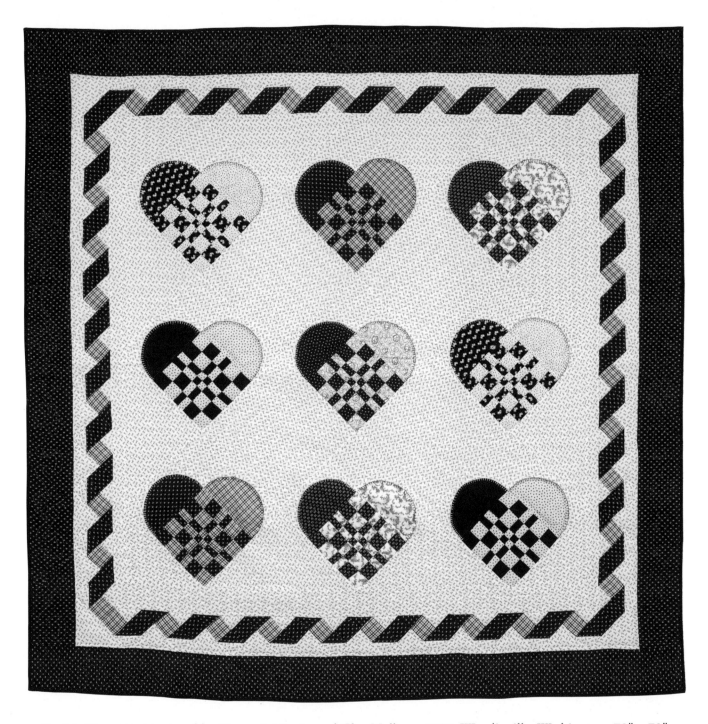

BE MY VALENTINE, pieced by Nancy J. Martin and Cleo Nollette, 1997, Woodinville, Washington, 73" x 73".
The strip-pieced hearts are based on a woven-paper design shown to Nancy by one of her Danish friends.
Each heart requires only one set of strips for the woven portion.
A twisted ribbon border complements the gentle curves.
Quilted by Mabel Beechy.

8. Make 2 ribbon borders as shown for the sides of the quilt.

Make 1.   Make 8.   Make 1.

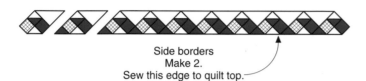

Side borders
Make 2.
Sew this edge to quilt top.

9. Stitch the borders to the sides, top, and bottom of the quilt, matching corner-square colors. Begin and end the stitching ¼" from the corners of the quilt, leaving the seam at the corner open.

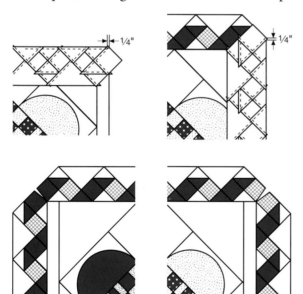

10. Stitch the borders together at each corner.

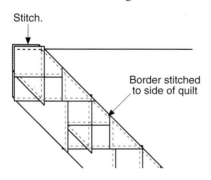

Stitch.

Border stitched
to side of quilt

11. Add the light-background triangles to the corners of the borders, trimming the excess if necessary.

12. Add the 5¼" x 63½" outer border strips to the sides of the quilt top, following the directions for borders on pages 66–67. Add the 5¼" x 73" outer border strips to the top and bottom of the quilt top.

13. Layer the quilt top with batting and backing. Tie or quilt. See the quilting suggestion below.

14. Bind the edges with the bias strips.

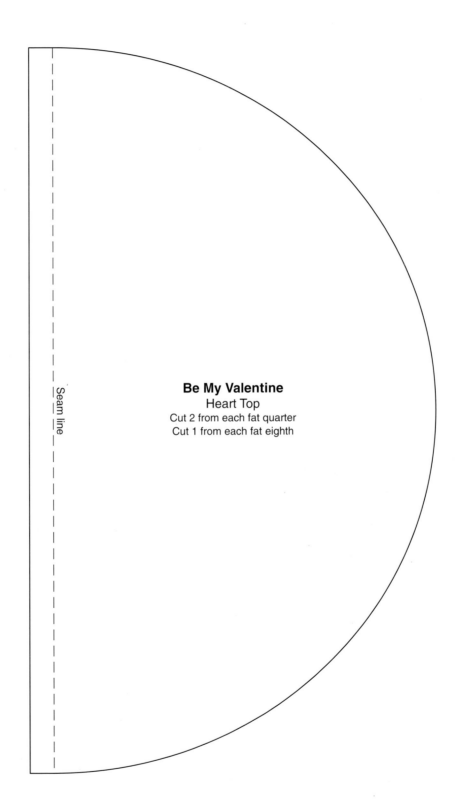

Seam line

Be My Valentine
Heart Top
Cut 2 from each fat quarter
Cut 1 from each fat eighth

Cake Stand

Cake Stand

DIMENSIONS: 67½" X 79"
FINISHED BLOCK SIZE: 8" X 8"

30 blocks, set diagonally with alternate blocks and side and corner setting triangles; pieced 5¾"-wide border and pieced corner blocks.

MATERIALS: 44"-WIDE FABRIC

¾ yd. each of 8 assorted light-background red fabrics for blocks and border

¾ yd. each of 8 assorted dark-background red fabrics for cake stands, alternate blocks, setting triangles, and border

4¼ yds. fabric for backing (crosswise join)

⅝ yd. fabric for 304" (8½ yds.) of bias binding

CUTTING
ALL MEASUREMENTS INCLUDE ¼"-WIDE SEAMS.

From EACH light-background red fabric, cut:

2 squares (16 total), each 8" x 8", for bias squares.

1 square, 8⅞" x 8⅞". Cut an additional 8⅞" square from one of the light fabrics, for a total of 9 squares. Cut the squares once diagonally to make 18 triangles for the pieced border.

4 squares (32 total), each 4⅞" x 4⅞". Cut once diagonally to make 64 triangles for blocks. You will use 60 and have 4 left over.

8 rectangles (64 total), each 2½" x 4½", for background. You will use 60 and have 4 left over.

4 squares (32 total), each 2½" x 2½", for blocks. You will use 30 and have 2 left over.

From the remaining light-background red fabrics, cut:

4 border corner pieces and 4 border corner pieces reversed, using the template on page 29.

From EACH dark-background fabric, cut:

2 squares (16 total), each 8" x 8", for bias squares. Pair each square with an 8" light-background square, right sides up. Cut and piece 2½"-wide bias strips, following the directions for bias squares on pages 57–59. Cut 120 bias squares, each 2½" x 2½". Combine the strips so that each Cake Stand block features a different combination of light and dark fabrics.

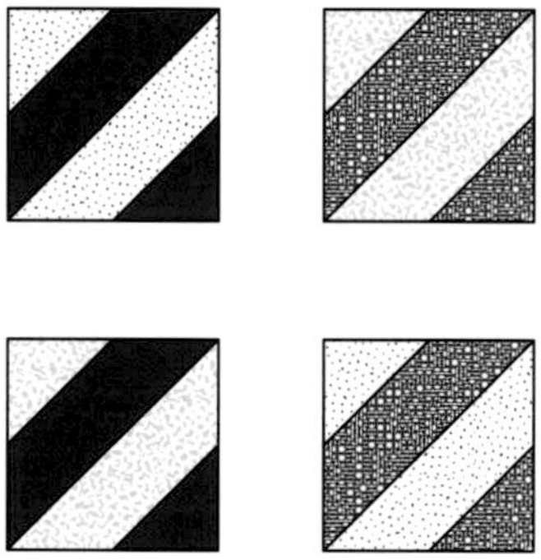

3 squares (24 total), each 8½" x 8½", for alternate blocks. You will use 20 and have 4 left over.

3 squares (24 total), each 8⅞" x 8⅞". Cut once diagonally to make 48 side setting triangles and pieced border triangles. You will use 40 and have 8 left over.

2 squares (16 total), each 4⅞" x 4⅞". Cut once diagonally to make 32 large triangles for blocks. You will use 30 and have 2 left over.

4 squares (32 total), each 2⅞" x 2⅞". Cut once diagonally to make 64 small triangles for blocks. You will use 60 and have 4 left over.

From the remaining dark-background fabrics, cut:

2 squares, each 6⅝" x 6⅝". Cut once diagonally to make 4 corner setting triangles.

2 squares, each 9⅜" x 9⅜". Cut once diagonally to make 4 triangles for pieced corners.

CAKE STAND, pieced by Cleo Nollette, 1997, Seattle, Washington, 67½" x 79".
Alternate blocks and a large-scale zigzag border highlight traditional Cake Stand blocks.
Quilted by Alma Miller.

DIRECTIONS

1. Using matching light- and dark-background pieces, join 4 bias squares, 1 light-background square, 1 light-background triangle, and 1 large dark-background triangle to make the upper section of the block. Make 30 sections.

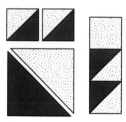
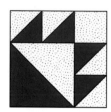

Make 30.

2. Join 2 small dark-background triangles, 2 light-background rectangles, and 1 light-background triangle to a section made in Step 1 to complete 1 Cake Stand block. Make 30 blocks.

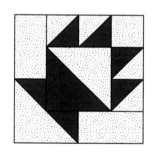

Make 30.

3. Join Cake Stand blocks, alternate blocks, and side setting triangles into diagonal rows. Join the rows. Add the corner setting triangles.

4. Join 5 light-background triangles and 6 dark-background triangles to make 2 side borders. Join 4 light-background triangles and 5 dark-background triangles to make the top and bottom borders. Add the borders to the quilt top. Handle the borders carefully because the outside edges are on the bias.

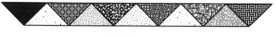

Side borders
Make 2.

Top and bottom borders
Make 2.

5. Join 2 border corner pieces and 1 large dark-background triangle to make 1 corner block. Make 4 corner blocks. Join the corner blocks to the quilt top, trimming them slightly if needed.

6. Layer the quilt top with batting and backing. Quilt or tie. See the quilting suggestion below.

7. Bind the edges with the bias strips.

¼" seam allowance

straight of grain

Cake Stand
Border Corner
Cut 4 and 4 reversed
from assorted light fabrics

Path to School

Schoolhouse

Single Irish Chain

DIMENSIONS: 78" X 78"
FINISHED SCHOOLHOUSE BLOCK: 10" X 10"
FINISHED SINGLE IRISH CHAIN BLOCK: 10" X 10"

25 blocks (12 Schoolhouse blocks and 13 Single Irish Chain blocks), set alternately with sashing and sashing squares; 8"-wide border.

MATERIALS: 44"-WIDE FABRIC

3½ yds. beige fabric for background
6 fat quarters of assorted red prints for schoolhouses
¼ yd. star print for windows and doors
2¾ yds. red fabric for Single Irish Chain blocks, sashing, and border
4½ yds. fabric for backing
⅝ yd. fabric for 320" (8⅞ yds.) of bias binding

CUTTING
ALL MEASUREMENTS INCLUDE ¼"-WIDE SEAMS.

NOTE
There are templates for Pieces 4–7 of the Schoolhouse block. The remaining pieces are rectangles or squares.

From the beige fabric for the background, cut:
78 squares, each 2½" x 2½", for Irish Chain blocks.
26 rectangles, each 2½" x 4½", for Irish Chain blocks.
26 rectangles, each 2½" x 6½", for Irish Chain blocks.
60 rectangles, each 2½" x 10½", for sashing.
24 rectangles, each 2½" x 1½", for Piece 1.
12 rectangles, each 4½" x 1½", for Piece 3.
12 Template 4 and 12 Template 4 reversed, using template on page 33.

12 Template 6, using template on page 33.
12 rectangles, each 1½" x 6", for Piece 10.
12 rectangles, each 1½" x 5½", for Piece 9.

From the star print for the doors and windows, cut:
12 rectangles, each 2½" x 4", for Piece 11.
24 rectangles, each 1½" x 3", for Piece 15.

From EACH of the 6 red prints* for the schoolhouses, cut:
4 squares (24 total), each 1½" x 1½", for Piece 2.
2 Template 5 (12 total), using template on page 33.
2 Template 7 (12 total), using template on page 33.
2 rectangles (12 total), each 1½" x 4½", for Piece 8.
8 rectangles (48 total), each 1½" x 5", for Piece 13.
2 rectangles (12 total), each 1½" x 2½", for Piece 12.
4 rectangles (24 total), each 1½" x 3½", for Piece 14.
2 rectangles (12 total), each 1½" x 3", for Piece 16.

* You will piece 2 Schoolhouse blocks from each red fabric.

From the red fabric for the Irish Chain blocks, sashing, and border, cut:
2 strips, each 8¼" x 62½", along the lengthwise grain, for side borders.
2 strips, each 8¼" x 78", along the lengthwise grain, for top and bottom borders.
153 squares, each 2½" x 2½", for Irish Chain blocks and sashing squares.

DIRECTIONS

1. Piece the sky/chimney and roof sections. Join the sections.

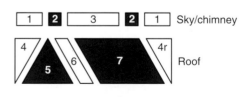

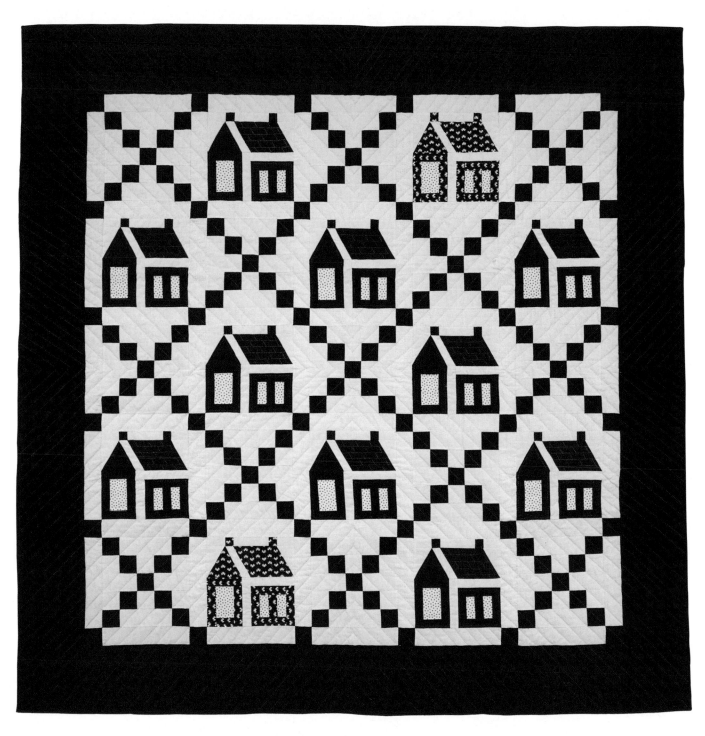

PATH TO SCHOOL, pieced by Cleo Nollette, 1997, Seattle, Washington, 78" x 78".
Single Irish Chain blocks create diagonal "paths" between Schoolhouse blocks
in this combination of traditional favorites. Quilted by Katie Yoder.

2. Piece the door section.

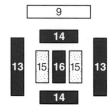

Door

3. Piece the window section.

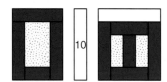

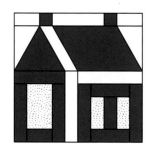

Window

4. Join the door and window sections, with Piece 10 in between.

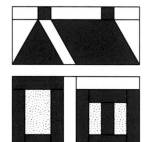

5. Join the sections to make 1 Schoolhouse block. Make 12 blocks.

Make 12.

6. Join the 4½"- and 6½"-long beige rectangles, beige squares, and 2½" red squares as shown into rows. Join the rows to make 1 Single Irish Chain block. Make 13 blocks.

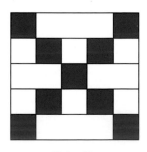

Make 13.

7. Join 5 sashing strips and 6 sashing squares for Row A. Make 6 of Row A.

8. Join 3 Single Irish Chain blocks and 2 Schoolhouse blocks with 6 sashing strips for Row B. Make 3 of Row B.

9. Join 3 Schoolhouse blocks and 2 Single Irish Chain blocks with 6 sashing strips for Row C. Make 2 of Row C. Join the rows.

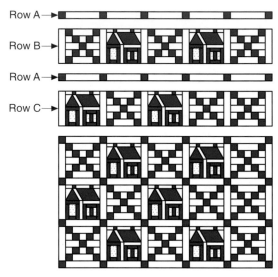

10. Add the 8¼" x 62½" border strips to the sides of the quilt top, following the directions for borders on pages 66–67. Add the 8¼" x 78" border strips to the top and bottom of the quilt top.

11. Layer the quilt top with batting and backing. Quilt or tie. See the quilting suggestion below.

12. Bind the edges with the bias strips.

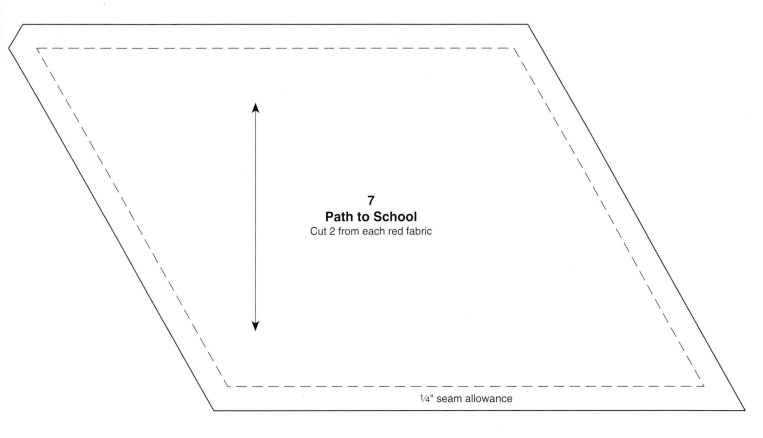

7
Path to School
Cut 2 from each red fabric

¼" seam allowance

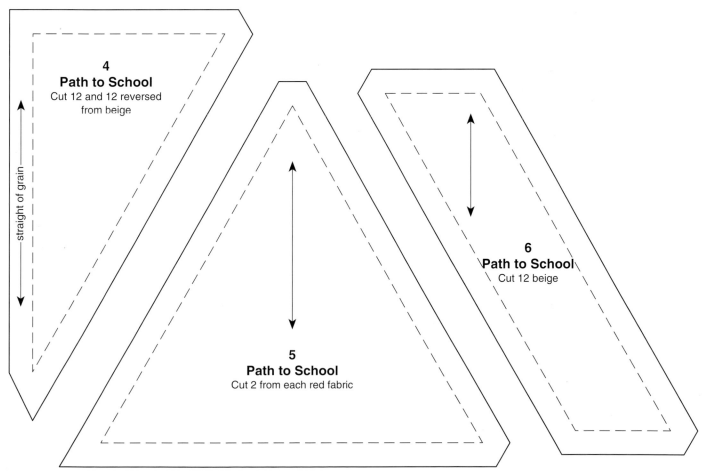

4
Path to School
Cut 12 and 12 reversed
from beige

straight of grain

5
Path to School
Cut 2 from each red fabric

6
Path to School
Cut 12 beige

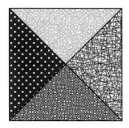

Frankly French

Sawtooth Star   Triangle Unit

DIMENSIONS: 81¼" x 81¼"

Center medallion, 25" x 25". Six borders surrounding the center medallion: 1½"-wide dark-background border; 2"-wide Sawtooth border; 8"-wide Sawtooth Star border; 1⅞"-wide light-background border; 5¾"-wide pieced-triangle border; and 9"-wide dark-background border.

MATERIALS: 44"-WIDE FABRIC

4½ yds. toile or scenic print for center medallion and outer borders*

⅞ yd. dark-background fabric for inner and pieced borders

1¼ yds. light-background fabric for middle and pieced borders

1 yd. each of 6 assorted prints for pieced borders

4⅞ yds. fabric for backing

¾ yd. fabric for 332" (9¼ yds.) of bias binding

* For a nondirectional print, you'll need 3⅛ yards.

CUTTING
ALL MEASUREMENTS INCLUDE ¼"-WIDE SEAMS.

From the toile or scenic print, cut:

2 strips, each 9¼" x 81¼", along the lengthwise grain, for side outer borders.

4 strips, each 9¼" x 42", along the crosswise grain, for top and bottom outer borders.**

1 square, 25½" x 25½", for center panel.

From the dark-background fabric, cut:

2 strips, each 2" x 25½", for dark inner border.

2 strips, each 2" x 28½", for dark inner border.

From the light-background fabric, cut:

6 strips, each 2⅜" x 42", for light middle border.

From the 6 assorted prints and remaining border fabrics, cut a total of:

8 squares, each 8" x 8", from light- and dark-background fabrics for bias squares. Pair the light and dark squares, right sides up. Cut and piece 2½"-wide bias strips, following the directions for bias squares on pages 57–59. Cut 56 bias squares, each 2½" x 2½".

From the remaining assorted prints and border fabrics, cut a total of:

20 squares, each 4½" x 4½", for centers of Sawtooth Star blocks.

80 squares, each 2⅞" x 2⅞". Cut once diagonally to make 160 triangles for Sawtooth Star points.***

84 squares, each 2½" x 2½", for corners of Sawtooth Star blocks*** and Sawtooth border.

20 squares, each 5¼" x 5¼". Cut twice diagonally to make 80 background triangles for Sawtooth Star blocks***.

40 squares, each 7" x 7". Cut twice diagonally to make 160 triangles for pieced-triangle units.

** For a nondirectional print, cut 8 crosswise strips, each 9¼" x 42".

*** To match fabrics for star points, corners, and background triangles, cut in multiples of 4 from each fabric.

FRANKLY FRENCH, pieced by Nancy J. Martin, 1997, Woodinville, Washington, 81¼" x 81¼".
Multiple borders and Sawtooth Stars, made mostly of French fabrics, surround a center panel of toile.
Yellows and greens, with bits of blue, balance the strong reds. Quilted by Alvina Nelson.

DIRECTIONS

1. Stitch the 2" x 25½" dark-background strips to the sides of the center panel. Stitch the 2" x 28½" dark-background strips to the top and bottom of the panel.

2. Join 14 bias squares, with 7 squares facing in each direction, to make 1 Sawtooth border strip. Make 4 strips. Add a 2½" square to each end of 2 of the border strips.

Make 2.

Make 2.

3. Stitch the shorter border strips to the sides of the quilt top. Stitch the longer border strips to the top and bottom of the quilt top.

4. Piece 20 Sawtooth Star blocks as shown. Within each block, use the same fabric for the star points, and matching fabric for the corners and background triangles.

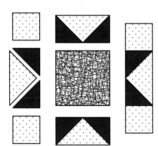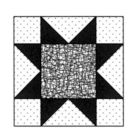

Make 20.

5. Piece 2 border strips with 4 Sawtooth Star blocks each, and 2 border strips with 6 Sawtooth Star blocks each.

6. Stitch the shorter border strips to the sides of the quilt top. Stitch the longer border strips to the top and bottom of the quilt top.

7. Piece the 2⅜"-wide light strips to make 4 strips for the middle border. Trim 2 strips to 48½". Trim the remaining 2 strips to 52¼". Stitch the shorter strips to the sides of the quilt top. Stitch the longer strips to the top and bottom of the quilt top.

8. Piece 40 triangle units as shown, mixing and matching a variety of prints in each unit.

Make 40.

9. Make 2 border strips, each with 9 triangle units, and 2 border strips, each with 11 triangle units.

Make 2.

Make 2.

10. Stitch the shorter border strips to the sides of the quilt top. Stitch the longer border strips to the top and bottom of the quilt top.

11. Piece the 9¼" x 42" outer border strips; trim to 63¾" and stitch to the top and bottom of the quilt top. Stitch the 9¼" x 81¼" outer border strips to the sides of the quilt top.

12. Layer the quilt top with batting and backing. Tie or quilt. See the quilting suggestion below.

13. Bind the edges with the bias strips.

Tree of Life

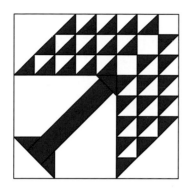

Tree of Life

DIMENSIONS: 84" x 84"
FINISHED BLOCK SIZE: 12" x 12"

13 blocks, set diagonally, with pieced sashing and sashing squares; side and corner setting triangles; 2"-wide inner border; 6"-wide outer border.

MATERIALS: 44"-WIDE FABRIC

6¼ yds. white tone-on-tone fabric for background, sashing strips, sashing squares, setting triangles, and outer border

3½ yds. red fabric for trees, sashing strips, sashing squares, and inner border

7½ yds. fabric for backing

¾ yd. fabric for 344" (9½ yds.) of bias binding

CUTTING
ALL MEASUREMENTS INCLUDE ¼"-WIDE SEAMS.

From EACH of the white tone-on-tone and red fabrics, cut:

4 fat quarters, each 18" x 22". Pair each white fat quarter with a red fat quarter, right sides up. Cut and piece 2"-wide bias strips, following the directions for bias squares on pages 57–59. Cut 312 bias squares, each 2" x 2".

From the remaining white tone-on-tone fabric, cut:

2 strips, each 6¼" x 72½", along the lengthwise grain, for outer side borders.

2 strips, each 6¼" x 84", along the lengthwise grain, for outer top and bottom borders.

13 squares, each 5⅜" x 5⅜". Cut once diagonally to make 26 large triangles for blocks.

39 squares, each 2" x 2", for blocks.

7 squares, each 3⅞" x 3⅞". Cut once diagonally to make 14 small triangles for blocks. You will use 13 and have 1 left over.

13 background template pieces and 13 template pieces reversed, using the template on page 41.

16 strips, each 1½" x 42", for sashing strips and sashing squares.

2 squares, each 22½ x 22½". Cut twice diagonally to make 8 side setting triangles.

2 squares, each 13¾" x 13¾". Cut once diagonally to make 4 corner setting triangles.

From the remaining red fabric, cut:

8 strips, each 2½" x 42", for inner borders.

59 squares, each 2⅜" x 2⅜". Cut once diagonally to make 118 triangles: 13 for top of trunk, 26 for base of trunk, and 78 for trees. You will have 1 triangle left over.

13 rectangles, each 1¾" x 7⅞", for tree trunks.

26 strips, each 1½" x 42", for sashing strips and sashing squares.

DIRECTIONS

1. Join 9 bias squares, 3 red triangles, and 1 large white triangle as shown to make the left section of the tree. Make a right section as shown. Make 13 of each section.

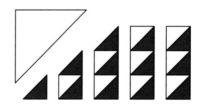

Left section
Make 13.

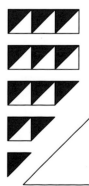

Right section
Make 13.

2. Join 6 bias squares and 3 white 2" squares as shown to make the top section of the tree. Make 13 sections.

Top section
Make 13.

3. Join 2 white background pieces, 3 red triangles, 1 small white triangle, and 1 red rectangle to make the center section of the tree. Make 13 sections.

Center section
Make 13.

4. Join the sections to make 1 Tree of Life Block. Make 13 blocks.

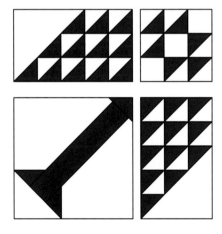

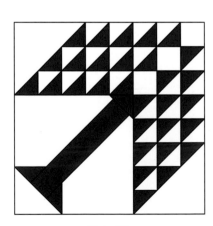

Make 13.

5. Join 2 red sashing strips and 1 white sashing strip to make Strip Set 1. Make 12 strip sets. Crosscut each set into 3 segments, each 12½" wide, for sashing, and 2 segments, each 1½" wide, for sashing squares. You should have a total of 36 long segments and 24 short segments.

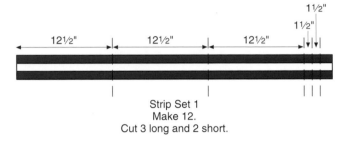

Strip Set 1
Make 12.
Cut 3 long and 2 short.

6. Join 2 white sashing strips and 1 red sashing strip to make Strip Set 2. Make 2 strip sets. Crosscut each set into 24 segments, each 1½" wide. You should have a total of 48 segments.

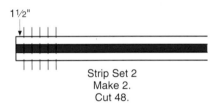

Strip Set 2
Make 2.
Cut 48.

7. Join the segments from Steps 5 and 6 to make a sashing square. Make 24 sashing squares.

Make 24.

8. Join a sashing strip to the right edge of each block.

Make 13.

38

TREE OF LIFE, pieced by Cleo Nollette, 1997, Seattle, Washington, 84" x 84".
Strip-pieced diagonal sashing and sashing squares add visual interest to this classic pattern.
Strong contrast between the red and white fabrics accentuates the graphic design. Quilted by Emma Raber.

9. Add additional sashing strips to the blocks and join the blocks into rows as shown. Make 2 rows of 1 block, 2 rows of 3 blocks, and 1 row of 5 blocks.

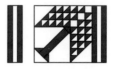

Make 2.

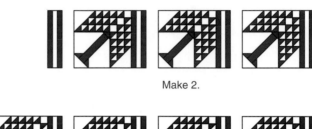

Make 2.

Make 1.

10. Join sashing strips and sashing squares into long sashing strips as shown. Make 2 rows of 1 strip and 2 squares, 2 rows of 3 strips and 4 squares, and 2 rows of 5 strips and 6 squares.

Make 2.

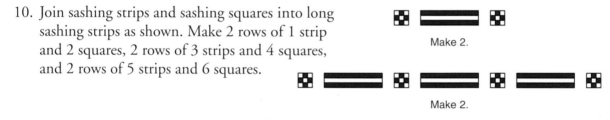

Make 2.

Make 2.

11. Sew the sashing strips to the rows of blocks as shown, sewing a long strip to each edge of the longest row. Add the side setting triangles. Join the rows. Add the corner setting triangles.

12. Piece and add the 2½"-wide red strips for the inner border, following the directions for borders on pages 66–67.

13. Add the 6¼" x 72½" white outer border strips to the sides of the quilt top. Add the 6¼" x 84" white outer border strips to the top and bottom of the quilt top.

14. Layer the quilt top with batting and backing. Quilt or tie. See the quilting suggestion below.

15. Bind the edges with the bias strips.

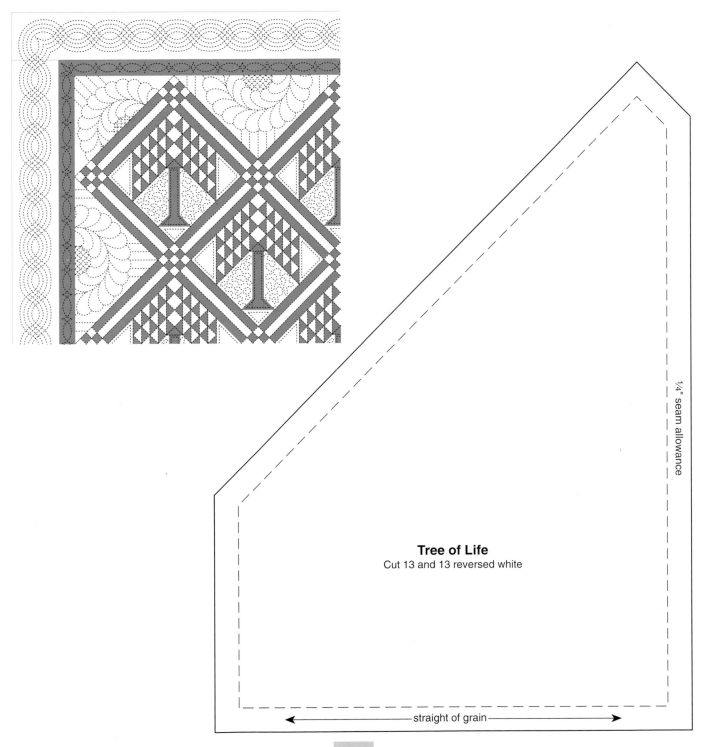

Tree of Life
Cut 13 and 13 reversed white

¼" seam allowance

← straight of grain →

Feathered Star

Feathered Star

DIMENSIONS: 76" x 76"
FINISHED BLOCK SIZE: 19" x 19"

NOTE
To eliminate unnecessary seams, you will construct this quilt in units, as a bar quilt. Then you will join the units into rows, rather than blocks.

9 blocks, set in bars with 3 stars across and 3 down; 1½"-wide inner border, 2"-wide Sawtooth middle border, and 6"-wide outer border.

MATERIALS: 44"-WIDE FABRIC

5½ yds. tone-on-tone print for background and borders

3 yds. red print for Feathered Stars and Sawtooth border

4¾ yds. fabric for backing

⅝ yd. fabric for 314" (8¾ yds.) of bias binding

CUTTING
ALL MEASUREMENTS INCLUDE ¼"-WIDE SEAMS.

From the tone-on-tone print, cut:

8 strips, each 2" x 42", for inner border.

2 strips, each 6¼" x 64½", along the lengthwise grain, for outer side borders.

2 strips, each 6¼" x 76", along the lengthwise grain, for outer top and bottom borders.

5 fat quarters, each 18" x 22", for bias squares.

4 squares, each 6" x 6", for Unit III.

8 rectangles, each 6" x 11½", for Unit IV.

4 squares, each 11½" x 11½", for Unit V.

12 squares, each 6⅛" x 6⅛", for Piece E.

3 squares, each 9¼" x 9¼", for Piece F. Cut twice diagonally to make 12 triangles.

36 Template G and 36 Template G reversed, using the template on page 44.

36 squares, each 1⅞" x 1⅞". Cut once diagonally to make 72 triangles for Piece H.

4 squares, each 2½" x 2½", for Sawtooth border.

From the red print, cut:

5 fat quarters, each 18" x 22". Pair 3 red fat quarters with 3 tone-on-tone fat quarters, right sides up. Cut and piece 1¾"-wide bias strips, following the directions for bias squares on pages 57–59. Cut 216 larger bias squares, each 1⁹⁄₁₆" x 1⁹⁄₁₆" (or use Template B), and 216 smaller bias squares, each 1½" x 1½" (or use Template A). Be sure to keep the different bias squares separate.

Pair each of the remaining red fat quarters with a white fat quarter, right sides up. Cut and piece 2½"-wide bias strips. Cut 120 bias squares, each 2½" x 2½", for the Sawtooth border.

From the remaining red print, cut:

9 squares, each 8½" x 8½", for star center (Unit I).

36 squares, each 1⁹⁄₁₆" x 1⁹⁄₁₆" (or use Template B).

36 Template C and 36 Template C reversed, using the template on page 44.

36 squares, each 3⅞" x 3⅞". Cut once diagonally to make 72 triangles for Piece D.

DIRECTIONS

1. Piece 12 of Unit VI, following the piecing diagram.

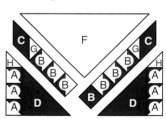 

Unit VI
Make 12.

FEATHERED STAR, pieced by Nancy J. Martin, 1997, Woodinville, Washington, 76" x 76".
Feathered Star blocks are assembled as a bar quilt, leaving plenty of open space for lavish quilting.
Quilted by Alvina Nelson.

2. Piece 12 of Unit II, following the piecing diagram.

E

C G G C
H B B H
A B B A
A B B A
A D D A
A B A

Unit II
Make 12.

3. Join the completed units to form bars. Join the bars as shown.

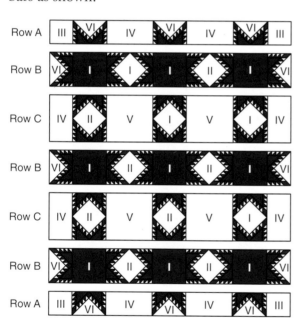

Row A III VI IV VI IV VI III
Row B VI I I I II I VI
Row C IV II V I V I IV
Row B VI I II I II I VI
Row C IV II V II V I IV
Row B VI I II I II I VI
Row A III VI IV VI IV VI III

4. Piece the 2"-wide tone-on-tone strips for the inner border. Add the borders, following the directions for borders on pages 66–67. The quilt top should measure 60½" x 60½".

5. To make the inner Sawtooth border, join 30 bias squares, each 2½" x 2½", with 15 facing in each direction. Make 4 strips. Add a 2½" square to each end of 2 of the strips. Add the strips to the quilt top.

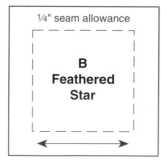

Make 2.

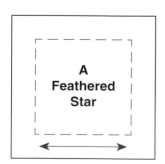

Make 2.

6. Add the 6¼" x 64½" border strips to the sides of the quilt top. Add the 6¼" x 76" border strips to the top and bottom of the quilt top.

7. Layer the quilt top with batting and backing. Quilt or tie. See the quilting suggestion below.

8. Bind the edges with the bias strips.

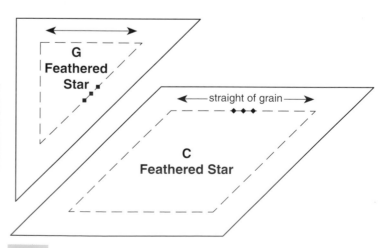

A
Feathered
Star

¼" seam allowance

B
Feathered
Star

G
Feathered
Star

straight of grain

C
Feathered Star

Essential Ingredients

ROTARY CUTTER AND MAT

A large rotary cutter enables you to quickly cut strips and pieces without templates. A cutting mat is essential to protect both the blade and table on which you are cutting. An 18" x 24" mat allows you to cut long strips, on the straight or bias grain. You might also consider purchasing a smaller mat to use when working with scraps.

Use a clear acrylic ruler to measure fabric and guide the rotary cutter. It is possible to cut quilt pieces with any see-through ruler that you have, and you can also adapt a general-purpose ruler to cut bias squares. It is easier, however, to use the special rulers that I recommend. They contain only the cutting lines and strategic alignment guides necessary to keep the fabric grain line in the correct position. Since you don't have to visually screen out unnecessary lines, your eyes can quickly focus on only the lines you need. Using a specialized ruler improves cutting accuracy, makes quiltmaking more fun, and frees you from the matching and stitching frustrations that can result from inaccurate cuts.

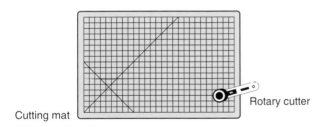

Cutting mat / Rotary cutter

ROTARY-CUTTING RULERS

Use a long, see-through ruler to measure and guide the rotary cutter. One that is 24" long is a good size. Try to find one that includes markings for 45° and 60° angles, guidelines for cutting strips, and standard measurements.

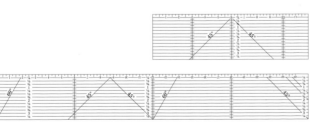

The Bias Square® ruler is critical for cutting accurate bias squares. This acrylic ruler is available in three sizes: 4", 6", or 8" square, and is ruled with ⅛" markings. A 20cm-square metric version is also available. All feature a diagonal line, which is placed on the bias seam, enabling you to cut two accurately sewn half-square triangles.

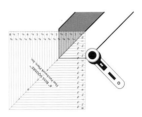

The Bias Square is also convenient to use when cutting small quilt pieces, such as squares, rectangles, and triangles. The larger 8" size is ideal for quick cutting blocks that require large squares and triangles as well as for making diagonal cuts for half-square and quarter-square triangles.

If the Bias Square is not available at your local quilt or fabric shop, you can order it from:

Martingale & Company
PO Box 118
Bothell, WA 98041-0118

You can also adapt a general-purpose rotary ruler to work in a similar fashion to the Bias Square.

1. Make a template by cutting a square of see-through plastic in the size specified for the bias square in the quilt directions.
2. Draw a diagonal line on the template, bisecting the square.
3. Tape the template to the corner of an acrylic ruler.

4. Follow the cutting directions given for the quilt you are making, substituting the template-adapted corner of the ruler for the Bias Square.

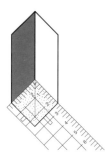

You will need to make a new template for each size bias square required for the quilt you are making. The most common sizes of bias squares are 2", 2½", and 3".

SEWING MACHINE

Stitching quilts on a sewing machine is easy and enjoyable. Spend some time getting to know your machine and become comfortable with its use. Keep your machine dust-free and well oiled.

Machine piecing does not require an elaborate sewing machine. All you need is a straight-stitch machine in good working order. It should make an evenly locked straight stitch that looks the same on both sides of the seam. Adjust the tension, if necessary, to produce smooth, even seams. A puckered seam causes the fabric to curve, distorting the size and shape of the piecing and the quilt you are making.

PINS

A good supply of glass- or plastic-headed pins is necessary. Long pins are especially helpful when pinning thick layers together.

If you plan to machine quilt, you will need to hold the layers of the quilt together with a large supply of rustproof, size 2 safety pins.

IRON AND IRONING BOARD

Frequent and careful pressing is necessary to ensure a smooth, accurately stitched quilt top. Place your iron and ironing board, along with a plastic spray bottle of water, close to your sewing machine.

NEEDLES

Use sewing-machine needles sized for cotton fabrics (size 70/10 or 80/12). You also need hand-sewing needles (Sharps) and hand-quilting needles (Betweens #8, #9, and #10).

SCISSORS

Use good-quality shears, and use them only for cutting fabric. Thread snips or embroidery scissors are handy for clipping stray threads.

SEAM RIPPER

This little tool will come in handy if you find it necessary to remove a seam before resewing.

Fabric Selection

YARDAGE REQUIREMENTS

As a quilting teacher, I have often seen the problems created by purchasing too little fabric. There is no flexibility to make the quilt bigger, to make a mistake, or to change your mind. So the fabric requirements given in this book are generous and based on yardage that is 42" wide after prewashing. If your fabric is wider than 42", there will be a little left over at the end of your strips. If your fabric is narrower than 42", you may need to cut an extra strip. Save any extra yardage or strips for future scrap quilts.

Many of the yardage amounts in this book specify fat quarters. This is an 18" x 22" piece of fabric rather than the standard quarter-yard that is cut selvage to selvage and measures 9" x 44". The fat quarter is a more convenient size to use, especially when cutting bias strips. Another common size is the fat eighth, which measures 9" x 22". Shops often offer the added convenience of fat quarters and fat eighths already cut and bundled. Look for the basket or bin of fat quarters and fat eighths when selecting fabrics.

FABRIC CHOICES

Many of these two-color quilts are created in a scrappy style, using an assortment of light-background fabrics and dark fabrics in reds or blues. Your fabric choices will depend on what appeals to you and what is available in your scrap bag.

If you have trouble selecting the red or blue prints for your color scheme, select a color-coordinated bundle of fat quarters or fat eighths. Often, this can be the basis for an effective color scheme with the purchase of additional background fabric. You can also purchase more of a particular fabric that you wish to predominate in your quilt. For instance, if the fabric requirements call for six dark fat quarters, you can purchase three fat quarters of a red print that you really like and one fat quarter of each of three other red prints.

Many of the quilts shown in this book use a combination of fabrics similar in color and value for the background. If you prefer the look of a single light background fabric, convert yardage given in fat quarters to yards. To do so, divide the number of fat quarters by four. For example, fourteen fat quarters equals 3½ yards of fabric.

For best results, select lightweight, closely woven, 100% cotton fabrics. Fabrics with a polyester content may make small patchwork pieces difficult to cut and sew accurately.

Wash all fabrics first to preshrink, test for colorfastness, and get rid of excess dye. Continue to wash fabric until the rinse water is completely clear. Add a square of white fabric to each washing of the fabric. When this white fabric remains its original color, the fabric is colorfast. A cupful of vinegar in the rinse water can also be used to help set difficult dyes.

After washing, press fabric and fold into fourths lengthwise. Make straight cuts with the rotary cutter across each end. When using the length of fabric, make straight cuts from one end and bias cuts from the other end. Then fold the fabric to store it.

Make it a habit to wash and prepare fabrics after you purchase them. Then your fabric will be ready to sew when you are.

FABRIC PLACEMENT

It's best to select your background fabric before you choose your red or blue fabrics. Don't limit your background choices to solid colors, even though white or muslin is traditional. If you really want to use a solid-colored fabric for the background, consider a white or cream tone-on-tone to add highlights. But remember, solid-colored fabrics tend to emphasize mismatched seams and irregular quilting stitches. If you are a beginner and are still perfecting your piecing and quilting skills, select a print that will help hide minor imperfections.

You can also cut the background from a dark fabric and use a lighter fabric for the design pieces. "Path of Action" (page 78) is a good example of this design scheme. An assortment of dark fabrics forms

Unsuitable background fabrics

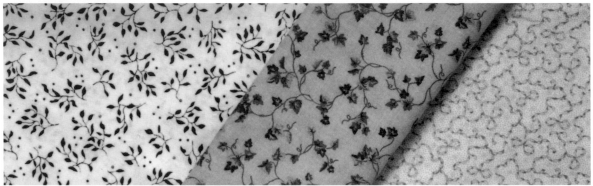

Suitable background fabrics

the background against which the light chain design appears.

Choose a background print that is nondirectional and still appears unified after being cut apart and resewn. Study the examples above for good and poor choices of background fabric.

To test the suitability of background fabrics while shopping, make several directional folds and evaluate the unity of the design.

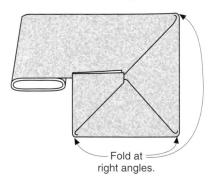

Fold at right angles.

Prints with a white background have a clean, formal look; those with a beige or tan background resemble antique quilts and have a more informal look.

Once you have chosen the background fabric, select remaining fabrics that will enhance it. Study the colors in the background-fabric design and begin your selection. When working with a single color family, such as blue, select a wide range of fabrics.

Begin with deep, dark navy blues, adding royal blues, medium blues, and light blues. If most of your blue fabrics are bright, stick to bright blues in all shades. If your blue fabrics are dull or "grayed," select muted shades of blue fabrics. Study the photo of "Aunt Sukey's Choice" (page 83) to see a wide range of fabrics.

If you work with scraps or fat quarters, you will use a number of different fabrics to represent a single value. When cutting the pieces shown as dark in the quilt plan, for example, you can use two, three, or ten different dark fabrics.

If you are using fabric randomly, don't worry about the placement of stripes or plaids. Let them fall as they are cut, including off-grain plaids. Stripes can be used horizontally and vertically in the same block.

Controlling the direction of striped fabric or directional prints requires careful cutting and placement. For example, in cutting half-square triangles, cut half the triangles in one direction and the remaining triangles in the opposite direction.

When sewing these pieces to a square or diamond, stitch the triangles from squares cut in one direction to opposite sides of the center square.

Then sew the pieces from squares cut in the opposite direction to the remaining sides of the center square.

To center a design from a pictorial or theme print, use a see-through ruler and adjust the crosswise cuts to center the design.

COMMON QUILT TERMS

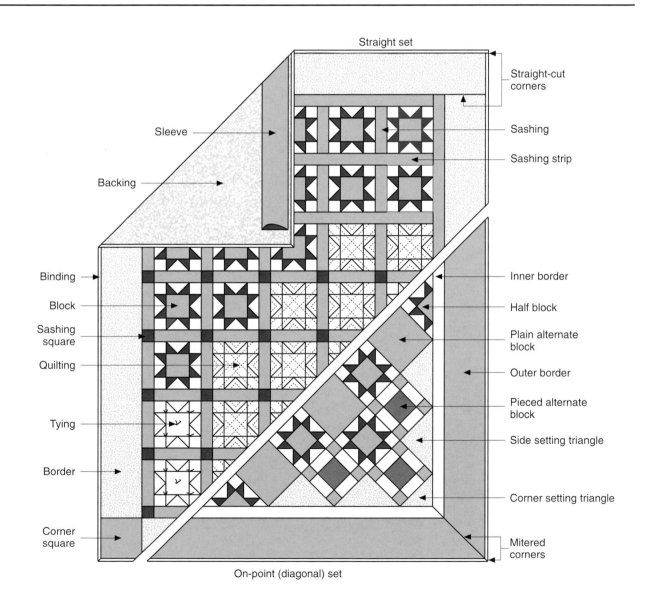

Rotary Cutting

USE AND CARE OF A ROTARY CUTTER

A rotary cutter has a *very sharp* blade. It is so sharp that you can cut yourself without even knowing it. If you are not extremely careful, you can also cut other people and objects that you had no intention of slicing. Before you use your rotary cutter for the first time, it is important to know some simple safety rules.

- Close the safety shield when the rotary cutter is not in use.
- Roll the cutter away from yourself. Plan the cutting so your fingers, hands, and arms are never at risk.
- Keep the cutter out of the reach of children.
- Dispose of used blades in a responsible manner. Wrap and tape cardboard around them before placing them in the garbage.

For comfort's sake, think about your posture and the table height as you cut. Stand to cut—you'll have more control than when sitting. Many quilters find they are more comfortable and can work longer if the cutting table is higher than a normal sewing table, so they don't have to bend as they cut. If you work on a table that is placed away from a wall, you can easily walk to another side of the table to make your next cut, rather than moving the fabric or the cutting mat.

If you are left-handed, reverse all cutting directions. Begin by placing the fabric to your left and the ruler to your right. Use a mirror to view the photos. This will help you see the proper cutting alignment.

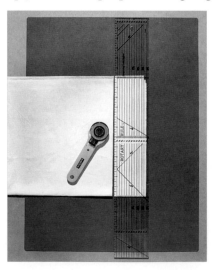

Remove the lint that builds up between the blade and the front sheath of your rotary cutter. Dismantle the cutter, paying close attention to how the pieces go together. Carefully wipe the blade with a soft, clean, cloth, adding a small drop of sewing-machine oil to the blade where it lies under the front sheath. Try this before changing to a new blade when the cutting action seems dull.

GRAIN LINES

Fabric is made of threads (called yarns) that are woven together at right angles. This gives fabric the ability to stretch or remain stable, depending on the grain line you use. The lengthwise grain runs parallel to the selvage and has little stretch, while the crosswise grain runs from selvage to selvage and has some give to it. Lines drawn at angles to the straight grain lines are considered bias. A true bias runs at a 45° angle to the lengthwise and crosswise grains.

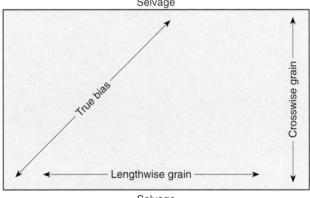

In most cases, the rotary-cutting directions use the following guidelines for grain-line placement:

- All strips are cut on the crosswise grain of fabric, unless otherwise noted.
- Squares and rectangles are cut on the lengthwise and crosswise grains of fabric.
- Half-square triangles are cut with the short sides on the straight grain and the long side on the bias. The Bias Square technique produces sewn half-square triangles whose grain lines follow this guideline.
- Quarter-square triangles have the short sides on the bias and the long side on the straight grain. They are generally used along the outside edges of the quilt, where the long edge will not stretch.
- The straight grain of fabric should fall on the outside edge of all pieced blocks.

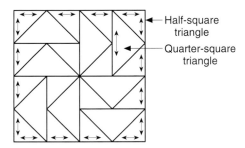

Half-square triangle

Quarter-square triangle

If fabric is badly off-grain, pull diagonally to straighten as shown.

Since many fabrics are printed off-grain, it is impossible to rotary cut fabrics exactly on the straight grain of fabric. In rotary cutting, straight, even cuts are made as close to the grain as possible. A slight variation from the grain will not alter your project.

CUTTING STRAIGHT STRIPS

Rotary cutting squares, rectangles, and other shapes begins with cutting strips of fabric. These strips are then crosscut to the proper dimensions. All strip measurements include ¼"-wide seam allowances.

To cut strips from the crosswise grain:

1. Fold and press the fabric with selvages matching, aligning the crosswise and lengthwise grains as much as possible. Place the folded fabric on the rotary-cutting mat, with the folded edge closest to your body. Align the Bias Square with the fold of the fabric and place a ruler to the left as shown.

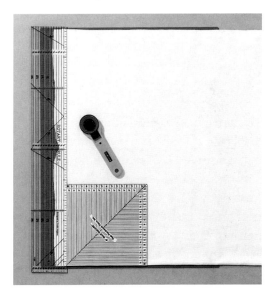

2. Remove the Bias Square and make a rotary cut along the right side of the ruler to square up the edge of the fabric. Hold the ruler down with your left hand, placing your little finger off the edge of the ruler to serve as an anchor and prevent slipping. Stand comfortably, with your head and body centered over your cutting. Do not twist your body or arm into an awkward position.

   As you cut, carefully reposition your hand on the ruler to make sure the ruler doesn't shift and the markings remain accurately placed. Use firm, even pressure as you cut. Begin rolling the cutter on the mat before you reach the folded fabric edge and continue across. For safety's sake, always roll the cutter away from you. Remember that the blade is very sharp, so be careful!

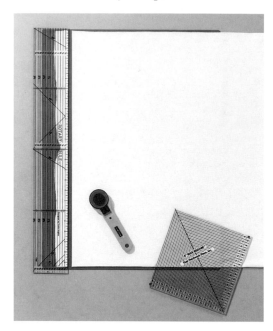

3. Fold the fabric again so that you will be cutting four layers at a time. Cut strips of fabric, aligning the clean-cut edge of the fabric with the ruler markings at the desired width. Open the fabric strips periodically to make sure you are cutting straight strips. If the strips are not straight, use the Bias Square to realign the ruler on the folded fabric, and make a fresh cut as in Steps 1 and 2 to square up the edge of the fabric before cutting additional strips. Don't worry. This adjustment is common.

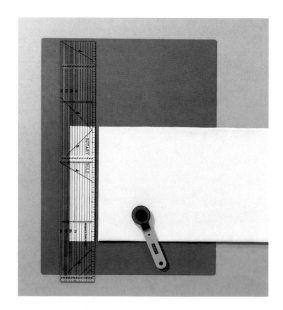

SQUARES AND RECTANGLES

1. Cut fabric into strips the measurement of the finished square plus seam allowances.

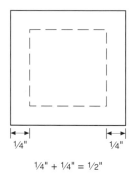

$$\frac{1}{4}" + \frac{1}{4}" = \frac{1}{2}"$$

2. Using the Bias Square, align the top and bottom edges of the strip and cut the fabric into squares the width of the strip.

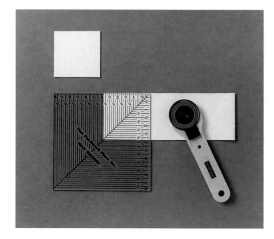

3. Cut rectangles in the same manner. First use the shorter measurement of the rectangle to cut strips, then use the longer measurement to cut the strips into rectangles.

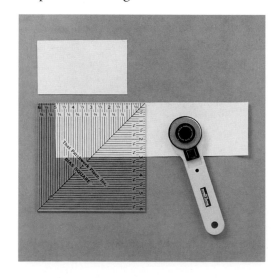

4. To cut a small, odd-sized square or rectangle for which there is no marking on your cutting guide, make an accurate paper template (including ¼"-wide seam allowances). Tape it to the bottom of the Bias Square, and you will have the correct alignment for cutting strips or squares.

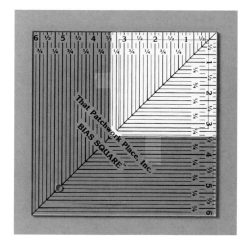

HALF-SQUARE TRIANGLES

Most of the triangles used in the quilts in this book are half-square triangles. These triangles are cut so that the straight grain is on the short edges of the triangle. Cut a square ⅞" larger than the finished size of the short edge of the triangle to allow for seam allowances; then cut the square once diagonally to yield two half-square triangles.

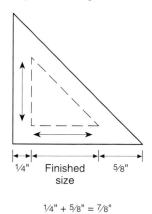

¼" Finished 5/8"
size

¼" + 5/8" = ⅞"

1. Add ⅞" to the desired finished size and cut a strip to this measurement.

2. Cut the strip into squares that are the same measurement as the strip width.
3. Cut a stack of squares once diagonally.

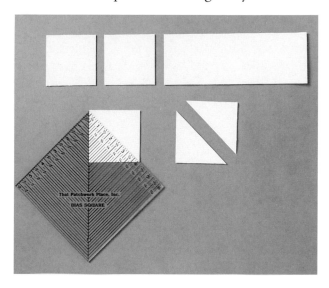

NUBBING CORNERS ON HALF-SQUARE TRIANGLES

Nubbing the corners on half-square triangles makes it easier to match edges precisely. Use the Bias Square to trim the corners. The example shown here is a half-square triangle with a finished dimension of 4".

1. To quick-cut this triangle, cut a 4⅞" square of fabric; then cut it once diagonally.
2. To trim the corners, add ½" to the finished size of the short side. Position the Bias Square's 4½" mark on the fabric triangle as shown. The points of the triangle will extend ⅜". Trim them off with the rotary cutter.

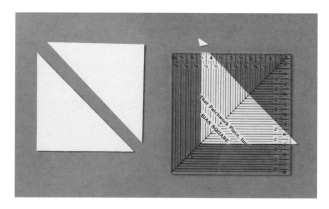

QUARTER-SQUARE TRIANGLES

These triangles are cut so that the straight grain is on the long edges of the triangles. The long sides are placed along the outside edges of blocks and quilts to keep the edges of quilts from stretching. Cut a square 1¼" larger than the finished size of the long edge of the triangle; then cut it twice diagonally to yield four quarter-square triangles.

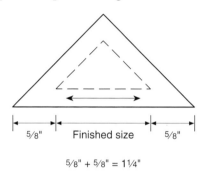

5/8" + 5/8" = 1¼"

1. Cut a strip as wide as the desired finished measurement plus 1¼".
2. Cut the strip into squares that are the same measurement as the strip width.
3. Cut a stack of squares twice diagonally.

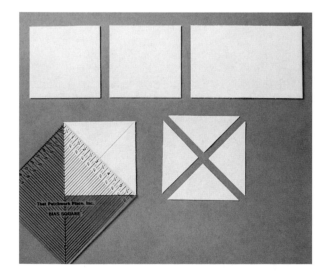

CUTTING BIAS STRIPS

To cut bias strips for binding:
1. Align the 45° marking of the Bias Square along the selvage and place the ruler's edge against it. Make the first cut.

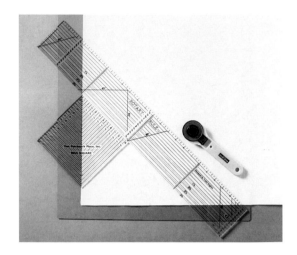

2. Measure the width of the strip from the cut edge of the fabric. Cut along the edge of the ruler.

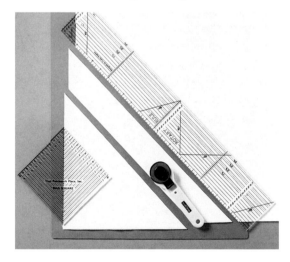

When cutting bias strips, a 24"-long ruler may be too short for some of the cuts. After making several cuts, carefully fold the fabric over itself so that the bias edges are even. Continue to cut bias strips.

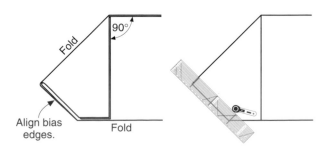

STRIP PIECING

Many of the quilts in this book contain simple units based on four-patch or nine-patch units. Strip piecing is a quick and easy way to mass-produce these units. It eliminates the long and tedious repetition of sewing individual pieces together.

To make four-patch or nine-patch units, first cut strips across the crosswise grain of fabric as shown on pages 51–52.

To determine the width to cut strips, add a ¼"-wide seam allowance to each side of the finished dimension on the desired shape. For example, if the finished dimension of a square will be 2", cut 2½"-wide strips. Strip widths given for all quilts include ¼"-wide seam allowances on each side.

FOUR-PATCH UNITS

1. Sew light and dark strips of fabric together with ¼"-wide seam allowances.
2. Press seam allowances toward the darker fabric, pressing from the right side so the fabric won't pleat along the seam lines. Usually, pressing toward the dark fabric will result in opposing seams.
3. Place these two sewn strips together with right sides facing, reversing the colors as shown. The seam allowances will face opposite directions.

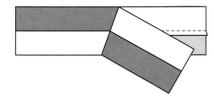

4. Cut sewn strips in pairs, beginning at the left side of the strip and working toward the right. The width of the cut is specified in the directions for each quilt.

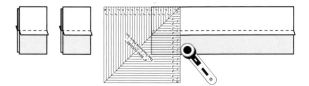

5. Stitch pairs together with ¼"-wide seam allowances to complete a four-patch unit. (See pages 62–63 for chain-piecing directions.)

6. Press seam to one side.

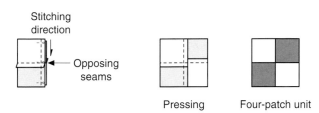

Stitching direction

Opposing seams

Pressing   Four-patch unit

NINE-PATCH UNITS

Nine-patch units are made using the same principle as four-patch units but with three strips of fabric instead of two. You need to make two different strip sets.

1. To make Strip Set 1, sew 1 light strip between 2 dark strips, using ¼"-wide seam allowances. Press seams toward the dark fabric.

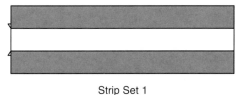

Strip Set 1
Make 2.

2. To make Strip Set 2, sew 1 dark strip between 2 light strips, using ¼"-wide seam allowances. Press seams toward the dark fabric.

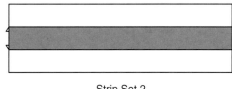

Strip Set 2
Make 1.

3. Place a Strip Set 1 and a Strip Set 2 together with right sides facing. The seam allowances will face opposite directions.

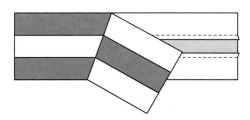

4. Cut strip sets in pairs. Begin at the left side of the strip and work toward the right. The width of the cut is specified in the directions for each quilt.

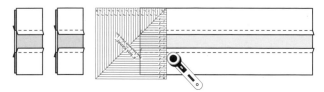

5. Stitch pairs together with ¼"-wide seam allowances. (See pages 62–63 for chain-piecing directions.)

6. Cut the remaining Strip Set 1 into pieces the same width as the pieces you cut for the pairs.
7. Stitch the remaining pieces to the previously sewn pairs to complete the nine-patch units.

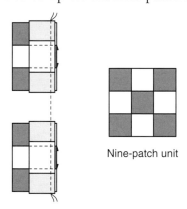

Nine-patch unit

8. Press seams as shown.

TIP

If you want strip-pieced units to contain a variety of fabrics instead of identical fabric combinations, vary the strips in the strip sets. Select a different combination of fabrics for each strip set and change the positions of the fabrics within the strip sets.

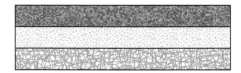

Strip Set 1

Strip Set 2

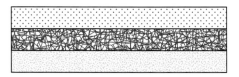

Strip Set 3

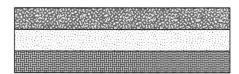

Strip Set 4

Your completed blocks will have a variety of scrappy fabric combinations.

BASIC BIAS SQUARE TECHNIQUE

Many traditional quilt patterns contain squares made from two contrasting half-square triangles. The short sides of the triangles are on the straight grain of fabric while the long sides are on the bias. These are called bias-square units. Using a bias strip-piecing method, you can easily sew and cut large amounts of bias squares. This technique is especially useful for small bias squares, where pressing after stitching usually distorts the shape (and sometimes burns fingers).

NOTE
All directions in this book give the cut size for bias squares; the finished size after stitching will be ½" smaller.

You will need to cut a sizable amount of bias squares for most of the quilts in this book. Use the technique shown below to help conserve time and fabric. Cut strips from fat quarters (18" x 22") or fat eighths (9" x 22") of fabric. The directions specify the fabrics to use and the width of the strips to cut.

1. Layer two pieces of fabric, right sides facing up, and cut as shown. Starting at the corner of the fabric, make the first cut at a 45° angle.

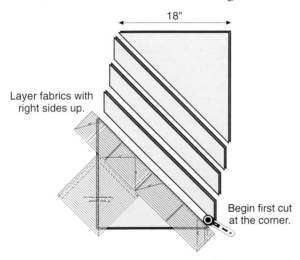

18"

Layer fabrics with right sides up.

Begin first cut at the corner.

2. Arrange the strips in the order you will sew them. Beginning with the triangular piece in either corner, select a strip from the top layer; then select the strip next to it from the bottom layer. Continue to select strips in this manner, alternating from the top and bottom layers as you move toward the opposite corner of the strips. This will give you two sets of strips to sew together.

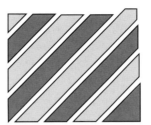 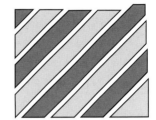

3. Sew the strips together along the long bias edge, right sides facing, with ¼"-wide seams. Offset the edges ¼" as shown.

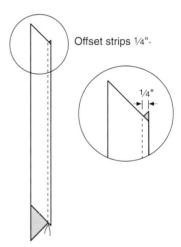

Offset strips ¼".

¼"

FAT QUARTERS CUTTING CHART FOR BIAS SQUARES
Based on 1 light and 1 dark fat quarter (18" x 22")

Strip Width	Cut Size of Bias Square	Yield	Finished Size of Bias Square
1¾"*	1½"	160	1"
2"*	1¾"	120	1¼"
2"	2"	100	1½"
2¼"	2¼"	80	1¾"
2½"	2½"	60	2"
2¾"	3"	50	2½"
3"	3½"	38	3"
3¾"	4½"	24	4"

* Press seams open rather than toward dark fabric.

The lower edge of the pieced rectangle and the adjacent side edge must form a straight line after sewing. The other two edges will be irregular. It is important to sew in this configuration if strip-pieced fabric is to yield the amount of bias squares indicated by the chart. Press seams toward the darker fabric. (If cutting bias squares 1¾" or smaller, try pressing the seams open to evenly distribute fabric bulk.)

The illustrations below show the strip-pieced fabric shapes that result when strips are stitched for the most common sizes.

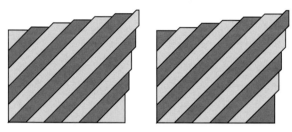

Strip-pieced fabric for 2½" cut (2" finished) bias squares

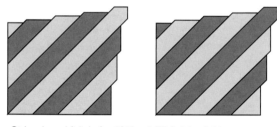

Strip-pieced fabric for 3½" cut (3" finished) bias squares

4. Begin cutting at the left side on the lower edge of each unit. Align the 45° mark of the Bias Square ruler on the seam line. Each bias square will require two cuts. The first cut is along the side and top edge. It removes the bias square from the rest of the fabric and is made slightly larger than the correct size, as shown in the series of illustrations below.

5. The second cut is made along the remaining two sides. It aligns the diagonal and trims the bias square to the correct size. To make the cut, turn the segment and place the Bias Square on the opposite two sides, aligning the required measurements on both sides of the cutting guide and the 45° mark on the seam. Cut the remaining two sides of the bias squares.

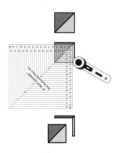

Turn cut segments and
cut opposite two sides.

6. Continue cutting bias squares from each unit in this manner, working from left to right and from bottom to top, row by row, until you have cut bias squares from all usable fabric. The chart on page 57 specifies how many bias squares you can expect to cut from two fat quarters (18" x 22") of fabric.

TIP
Remember, when cutting bias squares, if you don't have enough fabric to cut a 2½" bias square, cut a smaller size, such as 2¼" or 2", for use in another project. If you cut extra, smaller sizes of bias squares to finish off your bias-square strips, they will accumulate in no time, ready to make into a scrappy quilt.

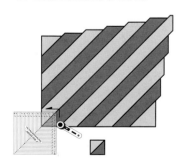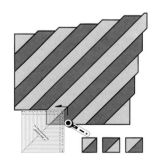

Align 45° mark on seam line and cut first two sides.

SCRAPPY BIAS SQUARES

For bias squares with a scrappy look, use a variety of fabrics when you make them. Layer four fat quarters of fabric in two pairs and cut into bias strips. Consult the cutting specifications for the quilt you are making to determine the strip width.

Mix and match the cut bias strips from the four fabrics to form rectangles and squares. Arrange and sew strips by size, placing the left and lower edges as straight as possible. The remaining edges will be uneven.

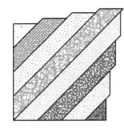
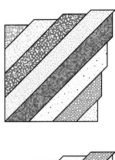
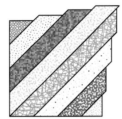
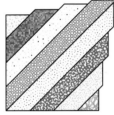

MAKING JUST A FEW BIAS SQUARES

If you don't need as many bias squares as a fat quarter yields, but you need more than one or two, start with small squares of fabric instead. Refer to the chart at right for common sizes and yields.

1. To make just a few bias squares, start with two small squares of fabric. Layer with right sides facing up and cut in half diagonally.

2. Cut into strips, measuring from the previous cut.

3. Stitch the strips together using ¼"-wide seam allowances. Be sure to align the strips so the lower edge and one adjacent edge form straight lines.

4. Starting at the lower left corner and following the directions on page 58, cut bias squares.

Use the chart below to determine strip width and resulting yield.

Finished Size	Cut Size	Fabric Size	Strip Width	Yield
2"	2½" x 2½"	8" x 8"*	2½"	8
2"	2½" x 2½"	9" x 9"	2½"	14
2½"	3" x 3"	8" x 8"	2¾"	8
3"	3½" x 3½"	9" x 9"	3"	8

* A pair of 7" x 7" squares will yield the same number of bias squares.

Machine Piecing

It's important to be comfortable with the sewing machine you are using. If this is your first machine-made quilt, practice guiding fabric through the machine. If you leave the machine unthreaded, you can practice over and over on the same pieces of fabric.

Operating a sewing machine requires the same type of coordination it takes to drive a car. You use your foot to control the machine's speed and your hands to control the fabric's direction. To start, use your right foot for the foot pedal to manage the speed. If the machine goes too fast at first, slip a sponge under a hinge-type pedal to slow it down. Use your hands to guide the fabric that feeds into the machine.

A good habit to develop is to use a seam ripper or long pin to gently guide the fabric up to the needle. You can hold seam intersections together or make minor adjustments before the fabric is sewn.

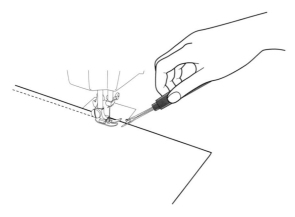

The most important skill in machine piecing is sewing an accurate ¼"-wide seam. This is necessary for seams to match and for the resulting block or quilt to measure the required size. There are several methods that will help you achieve this.

- Purchase a special foot that is sized so that you can align the edge of your fabric with the edge of the presser foot, resulting in a seam that is ¼" away from the fabric edge. Bernina has a special patchwork foot (#37), and Little Foot makes several special ¼" feet that fit most machines.

- If you have an electronic or computerized sewing machine, adjust the needle position so that the resulting seam is ¼" away from the fabric edge.
- Find the ¼"-wide seam allowance on your machine by placing an accurate template under the presser foot and lowering the needle onto the seam line; mark the seam allowance by placing a piece of masking tape at the edge of the template. You can use several layers of masking tape, building up a raised edge to guide your fabric. You can also use a piece of moleskin for a raised seam guide. Do the following test to make sure that the method you are using results in an accurate ¼"-wide seam.

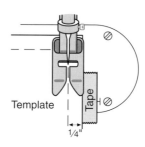

1. Cut 3 strips of fabric, each 1½" x 3".
2. Sew the strips together, using the edge of the presser foot or the seam guide you have made.
3. Press seams toward the outer edges. After sewing and pressing, the center strip should measure exactly 1" wide. If it doesn't, adjust the needle or seam guide in the proper direction.

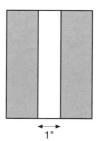

MATCHING SEAMS

When sewing the fabric pieces that make up a unit or block, follow the piecing diagram provided. Press each group of pieces before joining it to the next unit.

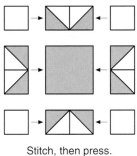

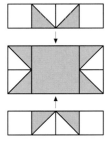

Stitch, then press.

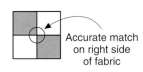

Join units together.

There are several techniques you can use to get your seams to match perfectly.

OPPOSING SEAMS: When stitching one seamed unit to another, press seams that need to match in opposite directions. The two "opposing" seams will hold each other in place and evenly distribute the fabric bulk. Plan pressing to take advantage of opposing seams. You will find this particularly important in strip piecing.

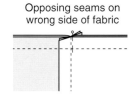

Opposing seams on wrong side of fabric

Accurate match on right side of fabric

POSITIONING PIN: A pin, carefully pushed straight through two points that need to match and pulled tight, will establish the proper matching point. Pin the remainder of the seam normally and remove the positioning pin just before stitching.

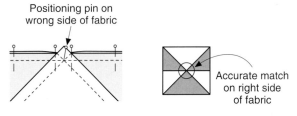

Positioning pin on wrong side of fabric

Accurate match on right side of fabric

THE X: When triangles are pieced, the stitches will form a X at the next seam line. Stitch through the center of the X to make sure the points on the sewn triangles will not be cut off.

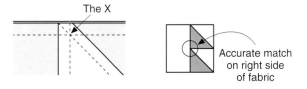

The X

Accurate match on right side of fabric

EASING: When two pieces you are sewing together are supposed to match but are slightly different in length, pin the points to match and stitch with the shorter piece on top. The feed dogs will ease the fullness of the bottom piece.

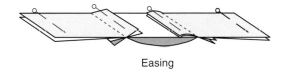

Easing

Inspect each intersection from the right side to see that it is matched. If the seams do not meet accurately, note which direction the fabric needs to be moved. Use a seam ripper to rip out the seam intersection and ½" of stitching on either side of the intersection. Shift fabric to correct the alignment, place positioning pins, then restitch.

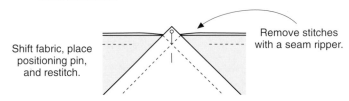

Shift fabric, place positioning pin, and restitch.

Remove stitches with a seam ripper.

PRESSING: After stitching a seam, it is important to press your work. Careful pressing helps make the next steps in the stitching process, such as matching points or aligning seams, easier.

Be sure to press, not iron, your work. Ironing is an aggressive back-and-forth motion that we use on clothing to remove wrinkles. This action can easily pull and distort the bias edges or seams in your piecing. Perfectly marked and sewn quilt pieces are commonly distorted by excessive ironing. You may notice this particularly after sewing what were two perfectly marked, cut, and sewn triangles into a square. Many times the finished unit is no longer square after you've ironed it. Pressing is the gentle lowering, pressing, and lifting of the iron along the length of the fabric without moving the iron back and forth along the seam. Let the heat, steam, and an occasional spritz of water press the fabric in the desired direction.

MATCHING BLOCKS

Rows of blocks should be pinned together at strategic intersections to ensure accurate matching as rows are sewn together. The process is similar to matching seams within a block.

To make this process easier, plan for opposing seams when you press blocks after stitching. Press seams in opposite directions from row to row.

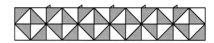

Row 1 — Press seams to right.

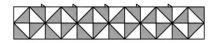

Row 2 — Press seams to left.

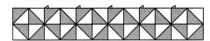

Row 3 — Press seams to right.

The points of carefully matched rows of blocks meet ¼" from the raw edge when rows are sewn together.

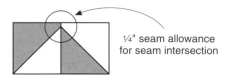

¼" seam allowance for seam intersection

Use positioning pins to hold seam allowances in place. Remove the pins before stitching through the seam intersection.

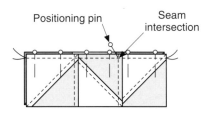

Positioning pin   Seam intersection

CHAIN PIECING

Chain piecing is an assembly-line approach to putting your blocks together. Rather than sewing each block from start to finish, you can sew identical units of each block together at one time, streamlining the process. It's a good idea, however, to first sew one sample block together from start to finish to ensure that the pieces have been accurately cut and that you have the proper positioning and coloration for each piece.

Stack the units you will be sewing in pairs, arranging any opposing seam allowances so that the top seam allowance faces toward the needle and the lower seam allowance faces toward you. Then you won't need to keep checking to see if the lower seam is being pulled to the wrong side by the feed dogs as you feed the fabric through the sewing machine.

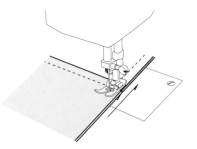

Face top seam allowance toward the needle whenever possible.

Feed units through the machine without stopping to cut thread. There will be a "stitch" or small length of thread between the units.

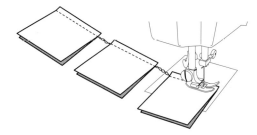

Take the connected units to the ironing board for pressing, then clip them apart. Chain piecing takes a little planning, but it saves you time and thread.

Use a "thread saver" to begin and end all your seams. Keep a stack of fabric scraps, about 2" x 2", near your machine. When you begin to sew, fold one of the squares in half and sew to its edge. Leave the presser foot down and continue sewing onto your piecing unit. When you have finished sewing a seam

or chain piecing, sew onto another thread saver, leaving the needle in place and the presser foot down. This thread saver will be in place for sewing the next seam or unit.

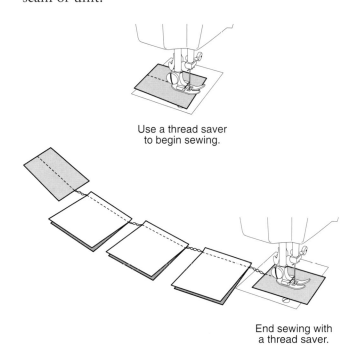

Use a thread saver
to begin sewing.

End sewing with
a thread saver.

This technique saves thread because you don't stop and pull a length of thread to remove fabric from the machine. All the tails of thread will be on the thread saver and not on the back of the block or quilt. This method also keeps the machine from eating the edges of the fabric as you start a seam.

Appliqué

"Be My Valentine" (page 21) and "Basket Stack" (page 84) have appliquéd accents. Following are directions for preparing and stitching the shapes.

PREPARATION

For the hearts in "Be My Valentine," use the paper-patch technique.

1. Make a template using the pattern on page 25 and plastic template material. Do not add seam allowances to the template.
2. On bond-weight paper or freezer paper, trace around the template to make a paper patch for each heart shape. Cut out the paper patch.
3. Pin or iron each paper patch to the wrong side of the fabric. If using freezer paper, pin with the plastic-coated side facing out.
4. Cut out each fabric shape, adding a ¼"-wide seam allowance along the curve only.
5. With your fingers, turn the seam allowance over the edge of the paper along the curve and baste to the paper. (You may wish to take small running stitches through the fabric near the edge of the curve first, to ease in the fullness.) Take an occasional stitch through the paper to hold the fabric in place.

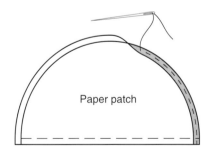

Paper patch

6. Press the appliqué pieces; then position and pin them in place on the background pieces.

For the handles in "Basket Stack," make the bias tubes as follows:

1. Fold each bias strip in half, wrong sides together, and stitch ⅛" from the edges. Press the tube so the seam falls on the back.

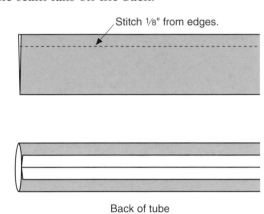

Stitch ⅛" from edges.

Back of tube

2. Position the placement template (page 87) on a background triangle. Align one edge of the bias tube with the template, forming a smooth curve. Pin or stitch in place.

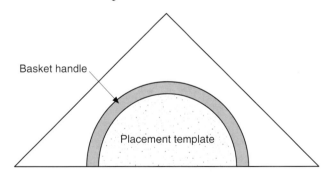

Basket handle

Placement template

APPLIQUÉ STITCH

Use a single strand of thread that matches the appliqué pieces to appliqué the hearts and the handles to the background fabric.

1. Start the first stitch from the back of the background fabric. Bring the needle up through the background fabric and through the folded edge of the appliqué piece.
2. Insert the needle next to where you brought it up, but this time put it through the background fabric only.
3. Bring the needle up through the background fabric and then into the appliqué piece, a little less than ⅛" from the first stitch. Space your stitches a little less than ⅛" apart.

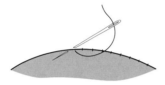

Appliqué stitch

4. For the heart shapes, slit the background fabric when the appliqué is complete and pull out the paper patch.

BUTTONHOLE STITCH

If you like, use a buttonhole stitch to embellish the edge of the heart shapes in "Be My Valentine."

1. Bring the needle up at A through the background fabric, just off the edge of the heart shape.
2. Take the needle down at B, inside the heart, and back out at C, just off the edge of the heart and over the thread.

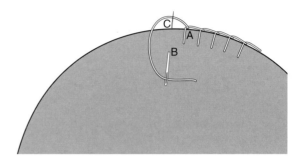

3. Repeat, keeping the stitches an even distance apart and an even distance into the heart.

You can also appliqué shapes by machine, using either invisible monofilament thread and a small zigzag stitch, or a machine buttonhole stitch if your machine has one. Consult your owner's manual and practice before you stitch your blocks.

Finishing Techniques

ADDING BORDERS

Borders can be used to frame and soften a busy design. They are also helpful in enlarging a quilt to fit a standard-size bed. It isn't always necessary to have a border on a quilt, however. Many antique quilts made from scraps have no borders, since continuous yardage was scarce and expensive.

Straighten the edges of your quilt top before adding borders. There should be little or no trimming needed for a straight-set quilt.

For many of the quilts in this book, you are instructed to cut lengthwise border strips to exact lengths. For other quilts, you will cut crosswise strips, piecing them as necessary, and then cut the borders to fit the quilt top.

To find the correct measurement for cut-to-fit border strips, always measure through the center of the quilt, not at the outside edges. This ensures that the borders are of equal length on opposite sides of the quilt and brings the outer edges into line with the center dimension if discrepancies exist. Otherwise, your quilt might not be "square" due to minor piecing variations and/or stretching that occurred while you worked with the pieces. If there is a large size difference between the two sides, it is better to go back and correct the source of the problem rather than try to make the border fit and end up with a distorted quilt.

STRAIGHT-CUT CORNERS

The easiest border to add is a straight-cut border. This method has been used on all the quilts with borders in this book. You will save fabric if you attach the border to the longer sides first, then stitch the border to the remaining two sides.

1. Measure the length of the quilt at the center. Cut two of the border strips to this measurement.

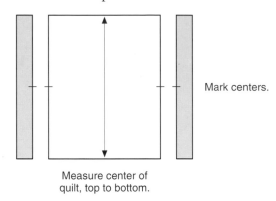

Mark centers.

Measure center of quilt, top to bottom.

If you cut borders on the crosswise grain, you may need to piece strips together before adding them to the quilt.

TIP
The seam will be less noticeable and stronger if it is pieced on an angle. You may need additional fabric to do so.

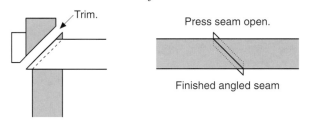

Trim.

Press seam open.

Finished angled seam

---

2. Mark the centers of the border strips and the quilt top. Pin the borders to the sides of the quilt, matching centers and ends and easing or slightly stretching the quilt to fit the border strip as necessary.
3. Sew the side borders in place and press the seams toward the borders.
4. Measure the center width of the quilt, including

the side borders, to determine the length of the top and bottom borders. Cut the border strips to this measurement, piecing strips as necessary. Mark the centers of the border strips and the quilt top. Pin borders to the top and bottom of the quilt top, easing or slightly stretching the quilt to fit as necessary.

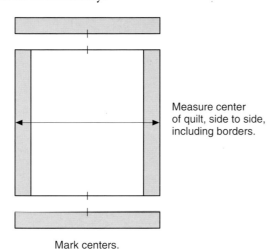

Measure center of quilt, side to side, including borders.

Mark centers.

5. Sew the top and bottom borders in place and press the seams toward the borders.

MARKING THE QUILTING DESIGN

Whether you machine or hand quilt, you'll need to mark a design to be quilted on the quilt top, unless you are stitching in-the-ditch, outlining the design ¼" from all seams, or stitching a grid of straight lines, using ¼"-wide masking tape as a guide.

To stitch in-the-ditch, place the stitches in the valley created next to the seam. Stitch on the side that does not have the seam allowance under it.

Quilting-in-the-Ditch

To outline a design, stitch ¼" from the seam inside each shape.

Outline quilting

To mark a grid or pattern of lines, use ¼"-wide masking tape in 15" to 18" lengths. Place strips of tape on a small area and quilt next to the edge of the tape. Remove the tape when stitching is complete. You can reuse the tape to mark another area.

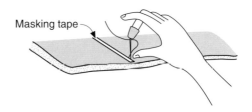

Masking tape

CAUTION
Don't leave tape on a quilt top for an extended length of time; it may leave a sticky residue.

To mark complex designs, use a stencil. Quilting stencils made from durable plastic are available in quilt shops. Use stencils to mark repeated designs. There is a groove cut into the plastic, wide enough to allow the use of a marking device. Just place the marker inside the groove to quickly transfer the design to the fabric. Good removable marking pencils include Berol silver pencils, EZ Washout marking pencils, mechanical pencils, and sharp regular pencils. Just be sure to draw lines lightly. Always test any marking device on a scrap of fabric for removability.

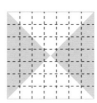 

Use a light table to trace more intricate designs. To make your own light table, separate your dining-room table as if adding an extra leaf. Then place a piece of glass, plastic, or Plexiglas over the opening. (I use the removable glass from a storm door for safety's sake, because there is a frame around the edge of the glass). Have the glass (or glass substitute) cut to fit your table at a glass shop, if desired, and frame or tape the edges to avoid cut fingers. For an additional fee, you can have glass edges finished to eliminate the sharp edges.

Once the glass is in place, position a table lamp on the floor beneath the table to create an instant light table. If your table does not separate, two card tables or end tables of the same height can be pushed together to create a support for the glass.

BACKING

For most quilts larger than crib size, you will need to piece the backing from two or more strips of fabric if you use 42"-wide fabric. Seams can run horizontally (crosswise join) or vertically (lengthwise join) in a pieced backing, as long as the fabric isn't a directional print. Avoid the temptation to use a bed sheet for a backing, as it is difficult to quilt through. Cut backing 3" to 4" larger than the quilt top all around. Be sure to trim away the selvages where pieces are joined.

Plan to put a sleeve or rod pocket on the back of the quilt so you can hang it. (See page 74.) Purchase extra backing fabric so that the sleeve and the backing match. Once you know the finished size of your quilt, refer to the following illustrations to plan the backing layout and to determine how much fabric you'll need.

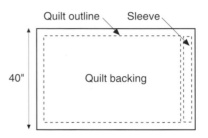

One fabric length:
For quilts up to 40" width or length
Example: 60" (length or width) +
18" (½ yd. for trimming and sleeve) =
78" (2⅛ yds.)

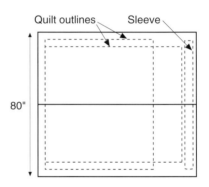

Two fabric lengths:
For quilts up to 80" width or length
Example: 2 x 100" (length or width) =
200" + 27" (¾ yd. for trimming and sleeve) =
227" (6⅓ yds.)

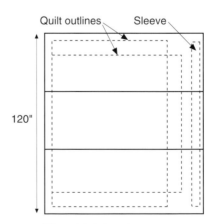

Three fabric lengths:
For quilts up to 120" width or length
Example: 3 x 100" = 300" + 36"
(1 yd. for trimming and sleeve) =
336" (9⅓ yds.)

Sometimes the backing fabric is a little too narrow for a 45"-wide quilt. Pieced backs are fun to make, and they can be the answer to this annoying problem.

For the upper quilt in the photo below, the checked backing was slightly narrow, so I trimmed a 6"-wide strip from one lengthwise edge. I then took leftover segments, bias squares, and partial blocks from the quilt front and pieced a 4"-wide strip. I stitched this pieced strip between the two sections of navy blue checked fabric, giving the backing a decorative touch while solving a problem.

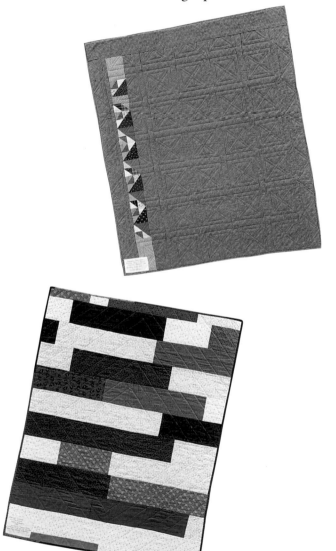

You can also use scraps of fabric from your sewing stash, piecing them together to form a backing large enough for your quilt top. This is most effective when you use some of the fabrics that were used on the front of the quilt.

BATTING

There are many types of batting to choose from. Select a high-loft batting for a bed quilt that you want to look puffy. Lightweight battings are fine for baby quilts or wall hangings. A lightweight batting is easier to quilt through and shows the quilting design well. It also resembles antique quilts, giving an old-fashioned look.

Polyester batting works well, doesn't shift after washing, and is easy to quilt through. It comes in lightweight and regular lofts as well as in a fat batting, or high loft, for comforters.

Cotton batting is a good choice if you are quilting an old quilt top. This batting must be quilted with stitches no more than 2" apart.

Dark batting works well behind a dark quilt top. If there is any bearding (batting fibers creeping through the top), it will not be as noticeable.

LAYERING AND BASTING

Open a package of batting and smooth it out flat. Allow the batting to rest in this position for at least twenty-four hours. Press the backing so that all seams are flat and the fold lines have been removed.

A large dining-room table, Ping-Pong table, or two large folding tables pushed together make an ideal work surface on which to prepare your quilt. Use a table pad to protect your dining-room table. The floor is not a good choice for layering your quilt. It requires too much bending, and the layers can easily shift or be disturbed.

Place the backing on the table with the wrong side of the fabric facing up. If the table is large enough, you may want to tape the backing down with masking tape. Spread your batting over the backing, centering it, and smooth out any remaining folds.

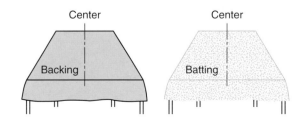

Center the freshly pressed and marked quilt top on these two layers. Check all four sides to make sure there is adequate batting and backing. Stretch the backing to make sure it is still smooth.

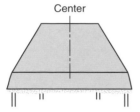

The basting method you use depends on whether you will quilt by hand or machine. Safety-pin basting is generally used for machine quilting, while thread basting is used for hand quilting.

THREAD BASTING

Starting in the middle of the quilt top, baste the three layers together with straight pins while gently smoothing out the fullness to the sides and corners. Take care not to distort the straight lines of the quilt design and the borders.

After pinning, baste the layers together with a needle and light-colored thread. (Dark-colored thread may bleed onto the quilt.) Start in the middle and make a line of long stitches to each corner to form a large **X**.

Continue basting in a grid of parallel lines 6" to 8" apart. Finish with a row of basting around the outside edges. Quilts that are to be quilted with a hoop or on your lap will be handled more than those quilted on a frame; therefore, they require more basting. After basting, remove the pins. Now you are ready to quilt.

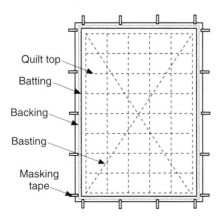

PIN BASTING

A quick way to baste a quilt top is with size 2 safety pins. They are large enough to catch all three layers but not so large that they snag fine fabric. Begin pinning in the center and work out toward the edges. Place pins 4" to 5" apart.

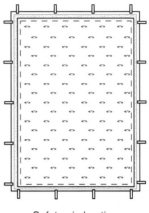

Safety-pin basting

Use long, straight pins along the outside edge to hold everything in place. Place pins perpendicular to the edge, 1½" to 2" apart.

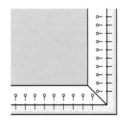

HAND QUILTING

To quilt by hand, you need quilting thread, quilting needles, small scissors, a thimble, and perhaps a balloon or large rubber band to help grasp the needle if it gets stuck. Quilt on a frame, a large hoop, or on your lap or a table. Use a single strand of quilting thread no longer than 18". Make a small, single knot at the end of the thread. The quilting stitch is a small running stitch that goes through all three layers of the quilt. Take two, three, even four stitches at a time if you can keep them even. When crossing seams, you might find it necessary to "hunt and peck" one stitch at a time.

To begin, insert the needle in the top layer about 1" from the point you want to start stitching. Pull the needle out at the starting point and gently tug at the knot until it pops through the fabric and is buried in the batting. Make a backstitch and begin quilting. Stitches should be tiny (eight to ten per inch is good), even, and straight; tiny will come with practice.

When you come almost to the end of the thread, make a single knot ¼" from the fabric. Take a backstitch to bury the knot in the batting. Run the thread off through the batting and out the quilt top; then snip it off. The first and last stitches will look different from the running stitches in between. To make them less noticeable, start and stop where quilting lines cross each other or at seam joints.

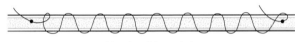

Hand quilting stitch

MACHINE QUILTING

Machine quilting is a good choice for those who have little time and need to finish their tops in a hurry. It's also a practical choice for baby quilts or other items that will be washed many times.

Machine quilting works best on small projects; it can be frustrating to feed the bulk of a large quilt through a sewing machine.

Use a walking foot or even-feed foot (or the built-in, even-feed feature, when available) for your sewing machine to help the quilt layers feed through the machine without shifting or puckering. This type of foot is essential for straight-line and grid quilting and for large, simple curves. Read the machine instruction manual for special tension settings to sew through extra fabric thicknesses.

Walking foot
attachment

Curved designs require free fabric movement under the foot of the sewing machine. This is called free-motion quilting, and with a little practice, you can imitate beautiful hand quilting designs quickly. If you wish to quilt curved designs with your machine, use a darning foot and lower the feed dogs while using this foot. Because the feed dogs are lowered for free-motion quilting, the speed at which you run the machine and feed the fabric under the foot determines the stitch length. Practice running the machine fairly fast, since this makes it easier to sew smoother lines of quilting. With free-motion quilting, do not turn the fabric under the needle. Instead, guide the fabric as if it were under a stationary pencil (the needle).

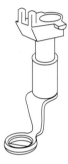

Darning foot

Practice first on a piece of fabric until you get the feel of controlling the motion of the fabric with your hands. Stitch some free-form scribbles, zigzags, and curves. Try a heart or a star. Then practice on a sample block with batting and backing. Make sure your chair is adjusted to a comfortable height. This type of quilting may feel awkward at first, but with a little determination and practice, you will be able to complete a project with beautiful machine quilting in just a few hours.

Keep the spacing between quilting lines consistent over the entire quilt. Avoid using complex, little designs and leaving large spaces unquilted. For most battings, a 2" or 3" square is the largest area that can be left unquilted. Read the instructions enclosed with the batting you have chosen.

Do not try to machine quilt an entire quilt in one sitting, even if it's a small quilt. Break the work into short periods, and stretch and relax your muscles regularly.

When all the quilting has been completed, remove the safety pins. Sometimes it is necessary to remove safety pins as you work.

BINDING THE EDGES

My favorite quilt binding is a double-layer French binding made from bias strips. It rolls over the edges of the quilt nicely, and the two layers of fabric resist wear. If you use 2¼"-wide strips, the finished width of this binding will be ⅜".

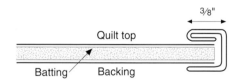

Double-Layer French Binding

The quilt directions tell you how much fabric to purchase for binding. If, however, you enlarge your quilt or need to compute binding fabric, use this handy chart:

Length of Binding	Fabric Needed
115"	¼ yd.*
180"	⅜ yd.
255"	½ yd.
320"	⅝ yd.
400"	¾ yd.
465"	⅞ yd.

It is a good idea to purchase ½ yard of fabric instead of ¼ yard so the bias strips will be longer and the binding won't have as many seams.

Determine the distance around your quilt and add about 10" for turning the corners and for overlapping the ends of the binding strips.

After quilting, trim excess batting and backing even with the edge of the quilt top. A rotary cutter and long ruler will ensure accurate straight edges. If the basting is no longer in place, baste all three layers together at the outer edges. If you are going to attach a sleeve to the back of your quilt for hanging, turn to page 74 and attach it now, before you bind the edges.

Follow these steps to bind the edges:
1. Cut 2¼"-wide bias strips as shown on page 54.
2. Stitch bias strips together, offsetting them as shown. Press the seams open.

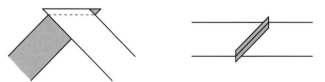

3. Fold the strip in half lengthwise, wrong sides together, and press.

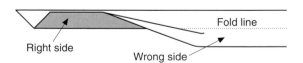

Right side   Wrong side   Fold line

4. Unfold the binding at one end and turn under ¼" at a 45° angle as shown.

Fold line

5. Beginning on one side of the quilt, stitch the binding to the quilt, using a ¼"-wide seam allowance. Start stitching 1" to 2" from the start of the binding. Stop stitching ¼" from the corner and backstitch.

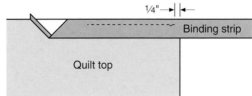

¼"

Binding strip

Quilt top

6. Turn the quilt to prepare for sewing along the next edge. Fold the binding away from the quilt as shown, then fold again to place the binding along the second edge of the quilt. (This fold creates an angled pleat at the corner.)

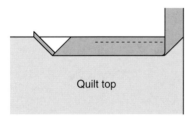

Quilt top

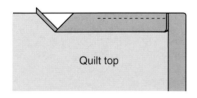

Quilt top

7. Stitch from the fold of the binding along the second edge of the quilt top, stopping ¼" from the corner as you did for the first corner; backstitch. Repeat the stitching and mitering process on the remaining edges and corners of the quilt.

8. When you reach the beginning of the binding, cut the end 1" longer than needed and tuck the end inside the beginning. Stitch the rest of the binding.

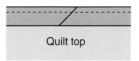

Quilt top

9. Turn the binding to the back side, over the raw edges of the quilt, and blindstitch in place, with the folded edge covering the row of machine stitching. At each corner, fold the binding as shown to form a miter on the back of the quilt.

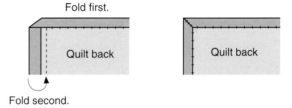

Fold first.

Quilt back

Quilt back

Fold second.

QUILT LABELS

It's a good idea to label a quilt with its name, the name and address of the maker, and the date it was made. Include the name of the quilter(s) if the quilt was quilted by a group or someone other than the maker. On an antique quilt, record all the information you know about the quilt, including where you purchased it. If the quilt is being presented to someone as a gift, also include that information.

To easily make a label, use a permanent-ink pen to print or legibly write all this information on a piece of muslin. Press freezer paper to the back of the muslin to stabilize it while you write. Press raw edges to the wrong side of the label. Remove the freezer paper and stitch the label securely to the lower corner of the quilt. You can also do labels in cross-stitch or embroidery.

QUILT SLEEVES

If you plan to hang your quilt, attach a sleeve or rod pocket to the back before attaching the binding. From the leftover backing fabric, cut an 8"-wide strip of fabric equal to the width of your quilt. You may need to piece two or three strips together for larger quilts. On each end, fold over ½" and then fold ½" again. Press and stitch by machine.

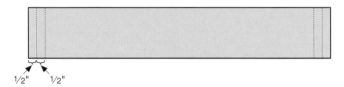

½"   ½"

Fold the strip in half lengthwise, wrong sides together; baste the raw edges to the top edge of the back of your quilt. These will be secured when you sew on the binding. Your quilt should be about 1" wider than the sleeve on both sides. Make a little pleat in the sleeve to accommodate the thickness of the rod, then slipstitch the ends and bottom edge of the sleeve to the backing fabric. This keeps the rod from being inserted next to the quilt backing.

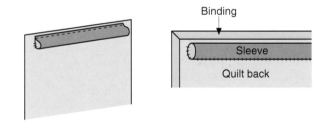

Binding
Sleeve
Quilt back

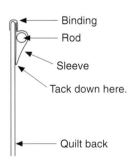

Binding
Rod
Sleeve
Tack down here.
Quilt back

THAT PATCHWORK PLACE TITLES:

All-Star Sampler • Roxanne Carter
Appliquilt® for Christmas • Tonee White
Appliquilt® to Go • Tonee White
Around the Block with Judy Hopkins
At Home with Quilts • Nancy J. Martin
Awash with Colour • Judy Turner
Baltimore Bouquets • Mimi Dietrich
Bargello Quilts • Marge Edie
*Basic Quiltmaking Techniques for Hand
    Appliqué* • Mimi Dietrich
Beyond Charm Quilts
    • Catherine L. McIntee & Tammy L. Porath
Blockbender Quilts • Margaret J. Miller
Block by Block • Beth Donaldson
Borders by Design • Paulette Peters
The Border Workbook • Janet Kime
The Cat's Meow • Janet Kime
Celebrate! with Little Quilts • Alice Berg,
    Mary Ellen Von Holt & Sylvia Johnson
Celebrating the Quilt
Class-Act Quilts
*Classic Quilts with Precise Foundation
    Piecing* • Tricia Lund & Judy Pollard
Color: The Quilter's Guide • Christine Barnes
Colourwash Quilts • Deirdre Amsden
Crazy but Pieceable • Hollie A. Milne
Crazy Rags • Deborah Brunner
Decorate with Quilts & Collections
    • Nancy J. Martin
Design Essentials: The Quilter's Guide
    • Lorraine Torrence
Design Your Own Quilts • Judy Hopkins
Down the Rotary Road with Judy Hopkins
Dress Daze • Judy Murrah
Dressed by the Best
The Easy Art of Appliqué
    • Mimi Dietrich & Roxi Eppler
Easy Machine Paper Piecing • Carol Doak
*Easy Mix & Match Machine Paper
    Piecing* • Carol Doak
Easy Paper-Pieced Keepsake Quilts
    • Carol Doak
Easy Paper-Pieced Miniatures
    • Carol Doak
Easy Reversible Vests • Carol Doak
Easy Seasonal Wall Quilts
    • Deborah J. Moffett-Hall
Easy Star Sampler • Roxanne Carter
A Fine Finish • Cody Mazuran
Freedom in Design • Mia Rozmyn
From a Quilter's Garden • Gabrielle Swain
Go Wild with Quilts • Margaret Rolfe
Go Wild with Quilts—Again! • Margaret Rolfe
Great Expectations • Karey Bresenhan
    with Alice Kish & Gay E. McFarland
Hand-Dyed Fabric Made Easy
    • Adriene Buffington
Happy Endings • Mimi Dietrich
Honoring the Seasons • Takako Onoyama
Jacket Jazz • Judy Murrah
Jacket Jazz Encore • Judy Murrah
The Joy of Quilting
    • Joan Hanson & Mary Hickey

Kids Can Quilt • Barbara J. Eikmeier
Life in the Country with Country Threads
    • Mary Tendall & Connie Tesene
Little Quilts • Alice Berg, Mary Ellen Von Holt &
    Sylvia Johnson
Lively Little Logs • Donna McConnell
Living with Little Quilts • Alice Berg,
    Mary Ellen Von Holt & Sylvia Johnson
The Log Cabin Design Workbook
    • Christal Carter
Lora & Company • Lora Rocke
Loving Stitches • Jeana Kimball
*Machine Needlelace and Other
    Embellishment Techniques* • Judy Simmons
Machine Quilting Made Easy • Maurine Noble
Machine Quilting with Decorative Threads
    • Maurine Noble & Elizabeth Hendricks
*Magic Base Blocks for Unlimited Quilt
    Designs* • Patty Barney & Cooky Schock
Make Room for Quilts (revised)
    • Nancy J. Martin
Miniature Baltimore Album Quilts
    • Jenifer Buechel
More Jazz from Judy Murrah
More Quilts for Baby • Ursula Reikes
More Strip-Pieced Watercolor Magic
    • Deanna Spingola
No Big Deal • Deborah L. White
Once upon a Quilt
    • Bonnie Kaster & Virginia Athey
Patchwork Pantry
    • Suzette Halferty & Carol C. Porter
A Perfect Match (revised)
    • Donna Lynn Thomas
Press for Success • Myrna Giesbrecht
Quick-Sew Celebrations
Quilted for Christmas, Book II
Quilted for Christmas, Book III
Quilted for Christmas, Book IV
Quilted Landscapes • Joan Blalock
Quilted Sea Tapestries • Ginny Eckley
A Quilter's Ark • Margaret Rolfe
Quilting Design Sourcebook • Dorothy Osler
Quilting Makes the Quilt • Lee Cleland
Quilting Up a Storm • Lydia Quigley
Quilts: An American Legacy • Mimi Dietrich
Quilts for Baby • Ursula Reikes
Quilts from Nature • Joan Colvin
QuiltSkills • The Quilters' Guild
Quilts Say It Best • Eileen Westfall
Rotary Riot • Judy Hopkins & Nancy J. Martin
Rotary Roundup
    • Judy Hopkins & Nancy J. Martin
Round Robin Quilts
    • Pat Magaret & Donna Slusser
Sensational Settings • Joan Hanson
Sew a Work of Art Inside and Out
    • Charlotte Bird
*Shortcuts: A Concise Guide to Rotary
    Cutting* • Donna Lynn Thomas
Show Me How to Paper-Piece • Carol Doak
Simply Scrappy Quilts • Nancy J. Martin
Small Talk • Donna Lynn Thomas
Soft Furnishings for Your Home
    • Sharyn Skrabanich
Square Dance • Martha Thompson
Stars in the Garden • Piece O'Cake Designs
Start with Squares • Martha Thompson

Strip-Pieced Watercolor Magic
    • Deanna Spingola
Stripples • Donna Lynn Thomas
Stripples Strikes Again! • Donna Lynn Thomas
Strips That Sizzle • Margaret J. Miller
Sunbonnet Sue All Through the Year
    • Sue Linker
Threadplay with Libby Lehman • Libby Lehman
The Total Bedroom • Donna Babylon
Traditional Quilts with Painless Borders
    • Sally Schneider & Barbara J. Eikmeier
Tropical Punch • Marilyn Dorwart
True Style • Peggy True
Two-Color Quilts • Nancy J. Martin
The Ultimate Book of Quilt Labels
    • Margo J. Clabo
Variations in Chenille • Nannette Holmberg
Victorian Elegance • Lezette Thomason
Watercolor Impressions
    • Pat Magaret & Donna Slusser
Watercolor Quilts
    • Pat Magaret & Donna Slusser
Weave It! Quilt It! Wear It!
    • Mary Anne Caplinger
Welcome to the North Pole
    • Piece O' Cake Designs
Whimsies & Whynots • Mary Lou Weidman
WOW! Wool-on-Wool Folk Art Quilts
    • Janet Carija Brandt
Your First Quilt Book (or it should be!)
    • Carol Doak

FIBER STUDIO PRESS TITLES:

*The Art of Handmade Paper and
    Collage* • Cheryl Stevenson
Complex Cloth • Jane Dunnewold
Dyes & Paints • Elin Noble
*Erika Carter: Personal Imagery
    in Art Quilts* • Erika Carter
*Fine Art Quilts: Work by Artists of the
    Contemporary QuiltArt
    Association*
Inspiration Odyssey • Diana Swim Wessel
The Nature of Design • Joan Colvin
Thread Magic • Ellen Anne Eddy
*Velda Newman: A Painter's Approach
    to Quilt Design* • Velda Newman with
    Christine Barnes

PASTIME TITLES:

*Hand-Stitched Samplers
from I Done My Best*
    • Saundra White
The Home Decorator's Stamping Book
    • Linda Barker
A Passion for Ribbonry • Camela Nitschke

Pastimes™

Many titles are available at your local quilt shop.
For more information, write for a free color catalog
to Martingale & Company, PO Box 118, Bothell,
WA 98041-0118 USA.

☎ U.S. and Canada, call **1-800-426-3126** for the
name and location of the quilt shop nearest you.
Int'l: 1-425-483-3313 • Fax: 1-425-486-7596
E-mail: info@patchwork.com
Web: www.patchwork.com   5.98

Two-Color Quilts

Ten True-Blue Quilts
from Nancy J. Martin

Martingale
& COMPANY

Bothell, Washington

TRUE-BLUE QUILTS

True-Blue Quilts

Path of Action

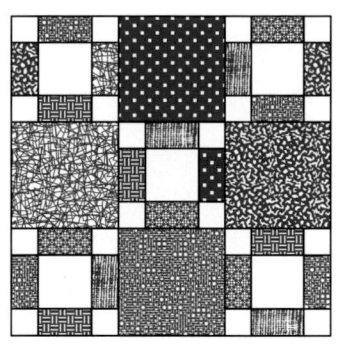

Path of Action

DIMENSIONS: 58" x 82"
FINISHED BLOCK SIZE: 12" x 12"

24 blocks, set 4 across and 6 down; 1"-wide inner border and 4"-wide outer border.

MATERIALS: 44"-WIDE FABRIC

⅜ yd. each of 10 assorted dark fabrics
¼ yd. each of 9 assorted light-background fabrics
½ yd. light fabric for inner border
1⅛ yds. dark fabric for outer border
3¾ yds. fabric for backing (crosswise join)
⅝ yd. fabric for 290" (8⅛ yds.) of bias binding

CUTTING
ALL MEASUREMENTS INCLUDE ¼"-WIDE SEAMS.

From the assorted dark fabrics, cut a total of:
16 strips, each 1½" x 42", for Strip Set 1.
9 strips, each 2½" x 42", for Strip Set 2.
11 strips, each 4½" x 42". Crosscut into 96 squares, each 4½" x 4½".

From the assorted light-background fabrics, cut a total of:
8 strips, each 2½" x 42", for Strip Set 1.
18 strips, each 1½" x 42", for Strip Set 2.

From the light fabric for the inner border, cut:
8 strips, each 1½" x 42".

From the dark fabric for the outer border, cut:
8 strips, each 4¼" x 42".

DIRECTIONS

1. Join two 1½" x 42" dark strips and a 2½" x 42" light strip to make Strip Set 1. Make 8 sets. Each set should measure 4½" wide when sewn. Crosscut the sets into 120 segments, each 2½" wide.

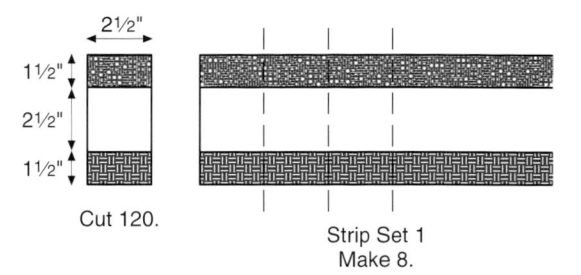

Cut 120.

Strip Set 1
Make 8.

2. Join a 2½" x 42" dark strip and two 1½" x 42" light strips to make Strip Set 2. Make 9 sets. Each set should measure 4½" wide when sewn. Crosscut the sets into 240 segments, each 1½" wide.

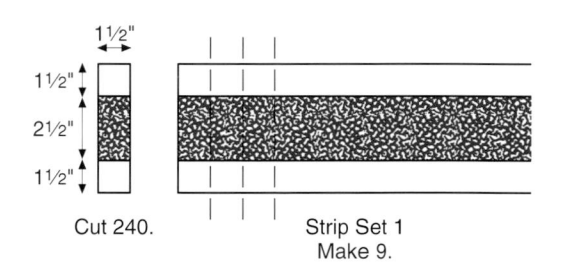

Cut 240.

Strip Set 1
Make 9.

3. Stitch the units together to make 120 Puss-in-the-Corner units.

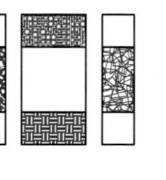 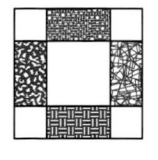

Make 120.

4. Join 5 Puss-in-the-Corner units and 4 dark 4½" squares to make 1 Path of Action block. Make 24 blocks.

  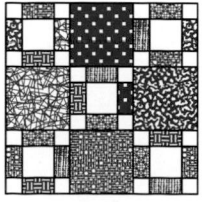

Make 24.

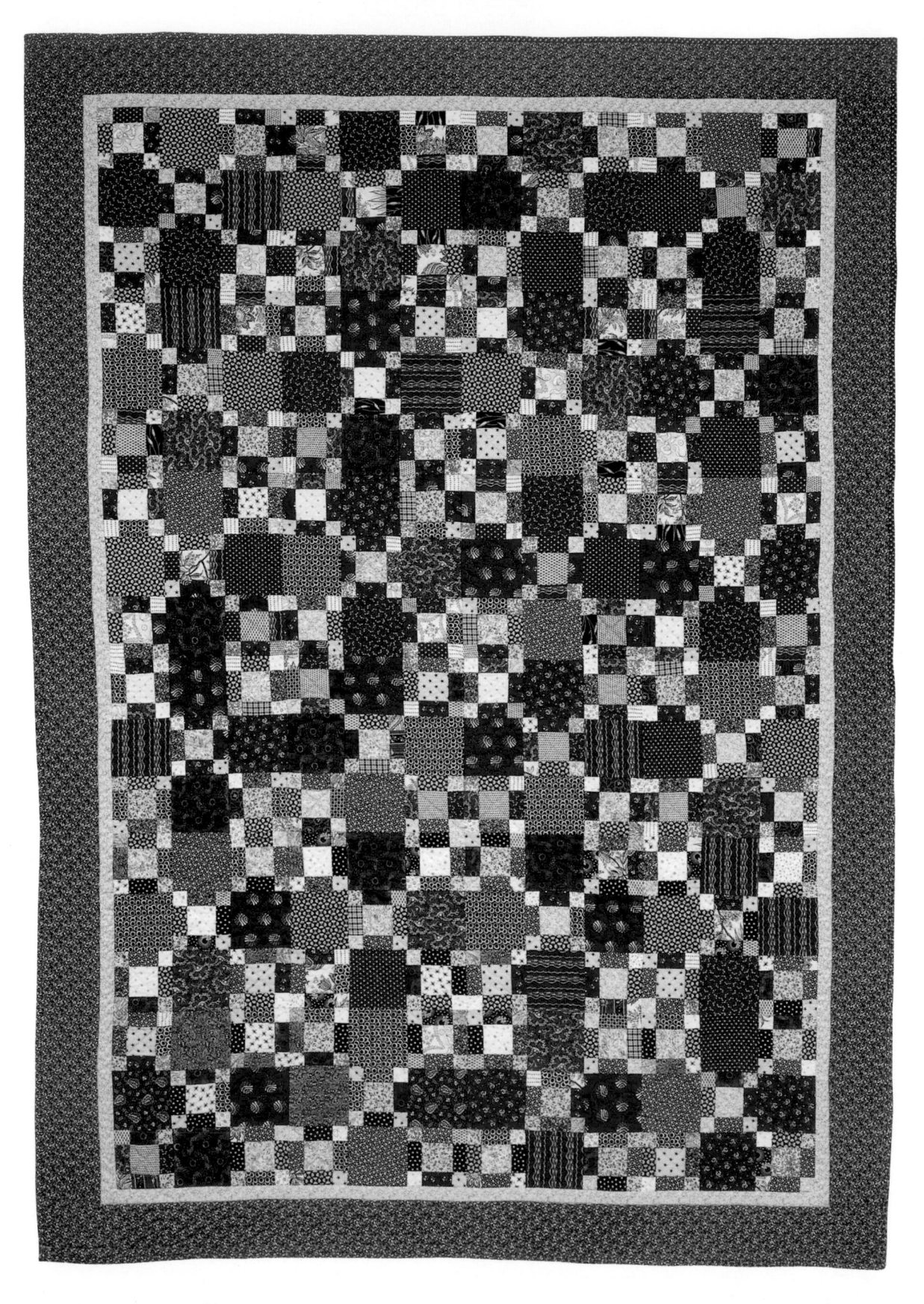

PATH OF ACTION, pieced by Nancy J. Martin and Cleo Nollette, 1997, Woodinville, Washington, 58" x 82". Reproduction indigo prints make up the five Puss-in-the-Corner units in each block of this scrappy quilt. Stitching the blocks together without sashing creates a chain pattern. Quilted by Celesta Schlabach.

5. Stitch the blocks into 6 rows of 4 blocks each. Join the rows.

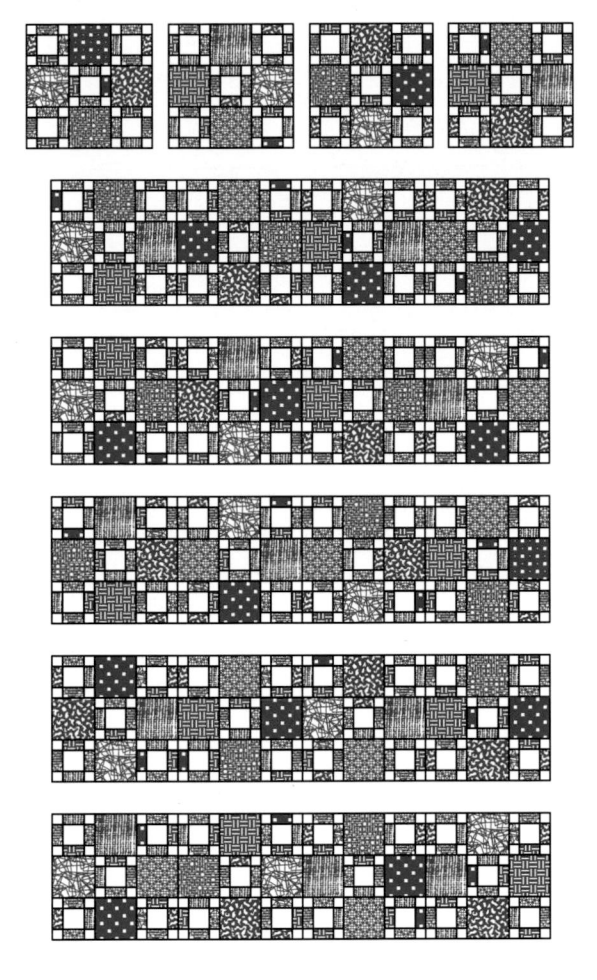

6. Add the 1½"-wide light strips for the inner border and the 4¼"-wide dark strips for the outer border, following the directions for borders on pages 66–67.
7. Layer the quilt top with batting and backing. Tie or quilt. See the quilting suggestion below.
8. Bind the edges with the bias strips.

Aunt Sukey's Choice

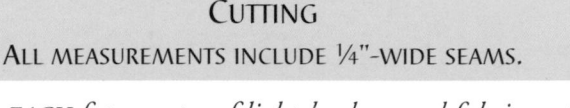

Aunt Sukey's Choice

DIMENSIONS: 44" X 58"
FINISHED BLOCK SIZE: 12" X 12"

12 blocks, set 3 across and 4 down, with 2"-wide sashing and sashing squares; optional button embellishment.

MATERIALS: 44"-WIDE FABRIC

10 fat quarters of assorted light-background fabrics for bias squares, sashing, and background*
6 fat quarters of medium-background fabrics for squares*
10 fat quarters of assorted dark-background fabrics for bias squares and triangles*
2¾ yds. fabric for backing (crosswise join)
½ yd. fabric for 212" (5⅞ yds.) of bias binding
128 buttons for tacking (optional)

If you have a large collection of scraps, don't hesitate to use additional pieces for a scrappier look as shown on page 83.

CUTTING
ALL MEASUREMENTS INCLUDE ¼"-WIDE SEAMS.

From EACH fat quarter of light-background fabric, cut:
2 squares (20 total), each 7" x 7", for bias squares.
4 strips (40 total), each 2½" x 12½", for sashing. You will use 31 and have 9 left over.
5 of Aunt Sukey's Choice template piece and 5 of template piece reversed (50 total and 50 total reversed). You will use 96 and have 4 left over.

From EACH fat quarter of medium-background fabric, cut:
28 squares (168 total), each 2½" x 2½", for blocks and sashing. You will use 164 and have 4 left over.

From EACH fat quarter of dark-background fabric, cut:
2 squares (20 total), each 5¼" x 5¼". Cut twice diagonally to make 80 triangles for blocks. You will use 48 and have 32 left over.
2 squares (20 total), each 7" x 7", for bias squares. Pair each square with a 7" square of light-background fabric; then cut and piece 2½"-wide bias strips, following the directions for bias squares on pages 57–59. Cut a total of 96 bias squares, each 2½" x 2½". You will be able to cut extra to mix and match fabrics.

DIRECTIONS

1. Join 4 medium squares to make a four-patch unit. Join 2 bias squares with matching light fabrics; repeat with 2 additional matching bias squares. Join the bias-square units and the four-patch unit.

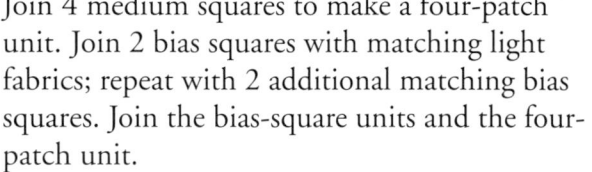
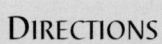
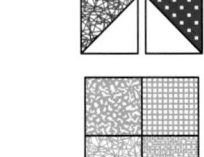
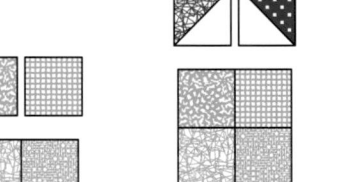
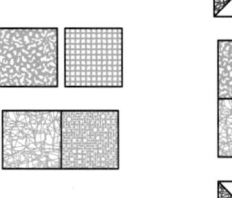
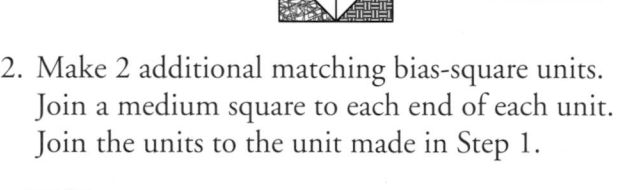

2. Make 2 additional matching bias-square units. Join a medium square to each end of each unit. Join the units to the unit made in Step 1.

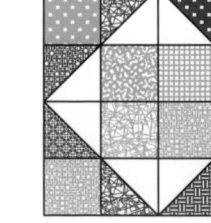

3. Join an Aunt Sukey's Choice template piece and a template piece reversed to a dark triangle. Make 4 units. Join a medium square to each end of 2 of the units.

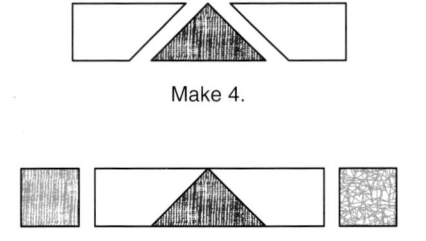

Make 4.

Make 2.

4. Join the units made in Steps 2 and 3 to make 1 Aunt Sukey's Choice block. Make 12 blocks.

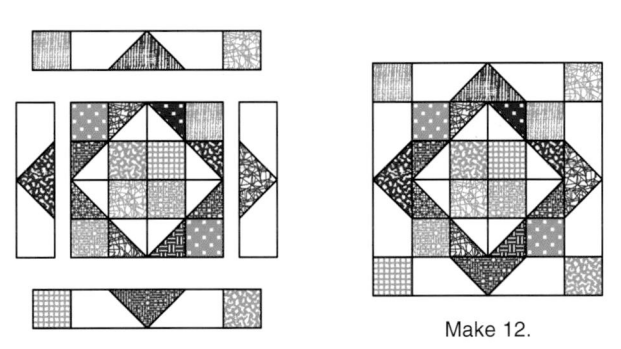

Make 12.

5. Join 3 blocks and 4 sashing strips to make a row. Make 4 rows.

Make 4.

6. Join 3 sashing strips and 4 sashing squares to make a sashing row. Make 5 sashing rows.

Make 5.

7. Join the rows, placing the long sashing strips between the rows as shown in the photo.

8. Layer the quilt top with batting and backing. Tie quilt or tack with buttons. See the tacking suggestion below. To tack with buttons, lower the feed dogs, adjust the stitch width, and bartack each button through all layers.

9. Bind the edges with the bias strips.

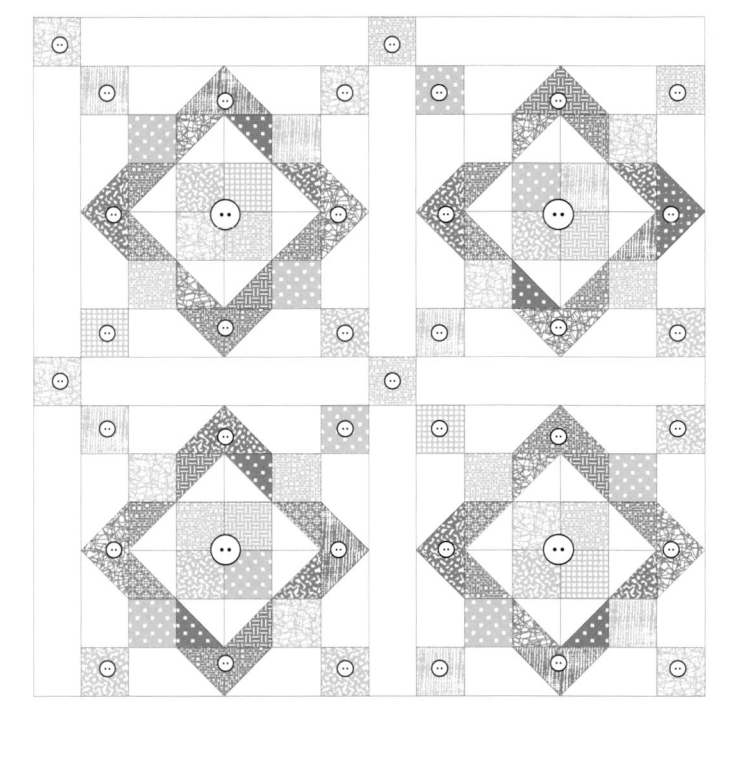

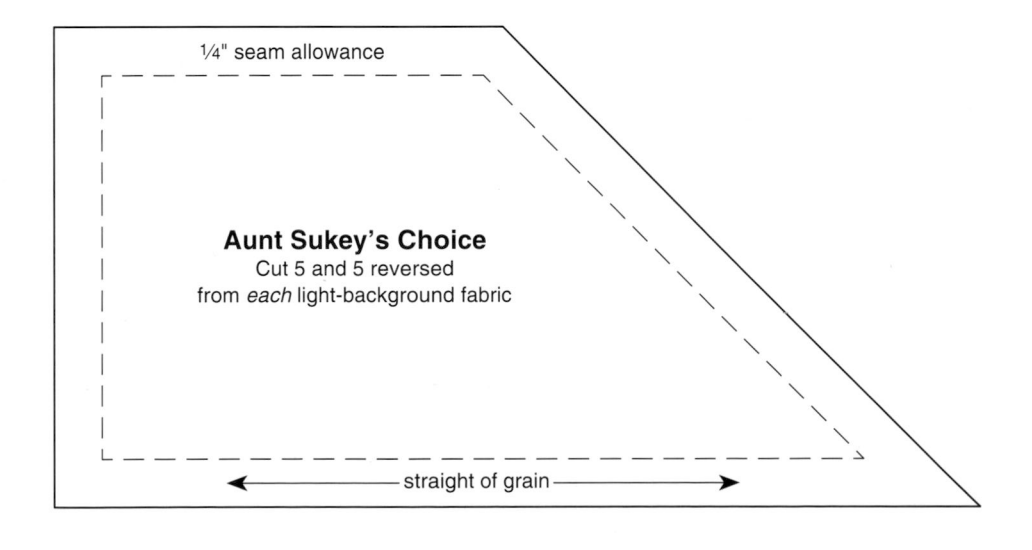

¼" seam allowance

Aunt Sukey's Choice
Cut 5 and 5 reversed
from *each* light-background fabric

◄──────── straight of grain ────────►

AUNT SUKEY'S CHOICE, by Nancy J. Martin and Cleo Nollette, 1997, Woodinville, Washington, 44" x 58".
Bright blue and white buttons embellish the surface and secure the layers of this scrappy quilt.

Basket Stack

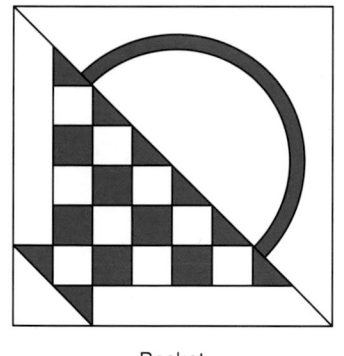

Basket

DIMENSIONS: 74" X 88"
FINISHED BLOCK SIZE: 8" X 8"

18 blocks, set on point, with 3 strips of 6 blocks each; 10"-wide sashing strips, and 10¼"-wide borders.

MATERIALS: 44"-WIDE FABRIC

6 fat quarters of indigo or dark navy blue fabrics
¾ yd. each of 6 light-background fabrics with navy blue prints
4¼ yds. large-scale print for sashing and borders
5¼ yds. fabric for backing (lengthwise join)
¾ yd. fabric for 332" (9¼ yds.) of bias binding

CUTTING
ALL MEASUREMENTS INCLUDE ¼"-WIDE SEAMS.

From EACH fat quarter of indigo or dark navy blue fabric, cut:
3 strips (18 total), each 1½" x 20".
12 squares (72 total), each 1⅞" x 1⅞". Cut once diagonally to make 144 triangles.
3 bias strips (18 total), each 1¼" x 13", for basket handles.

From EACH light-background fabric, cut:
3 strips (18 total), each 1½" x 20".
9 squares (54 total), each 1½" x 1½".
3 of Basket Stack template and 3 of template reversed (18 total and 18 total reversed).
2 squares (12 total), each 2⅞" x 2⅞". Cut once diagonally to make 24 small triangles. There will be 1 of each fabric left over.

2 squares (12 total), each 8⅞" x 8⅞". Cut once diagonally to make 24 large triangles. There will be 1 of each fabric left over.

From remaining light-background fabric, cut a total of:
8 squares, each 12⅝" x 12⅝". Cut twice diagonally to make 32 side setting triangles. You will use 30 and have 2 left over.
6 squares, each 6⅝" x 6⅝". Cut once diagonally to make 12 corner setting triangles.

From the large-scale print, cut:
4 strips, each 10½" x 68½", along the lengthwise grain, for vertical sashing and side borders.
2 strips, each 10½" x 74½", along the lengthwise grain, for top and bottom borders.

DIRECTIONS

1. Join 2 dark and 2 light strips, each 1½" x 20", to make Strip Set 1. The strip set should measure 4½" wide when sewn. Make 6 strip sets. Cross-cut each strip set into 6 segments, each 1½" wide, for a total of 36 segments.

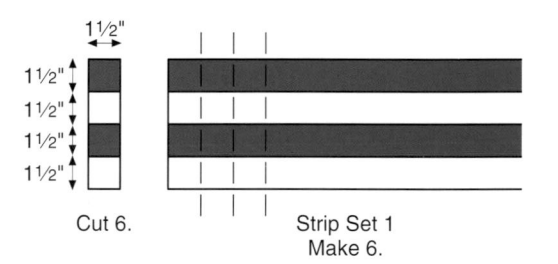

2. Join 1 dark and 1 light strip, each 1½" x 20", to make Strip Set 2. The strip set should measure 2½" wide when sewn. Make 6 strip sets. Cross-cut each strip set into 6 segments, each 1½" wide, for a total of 36 segments.

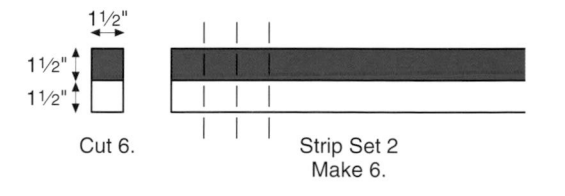

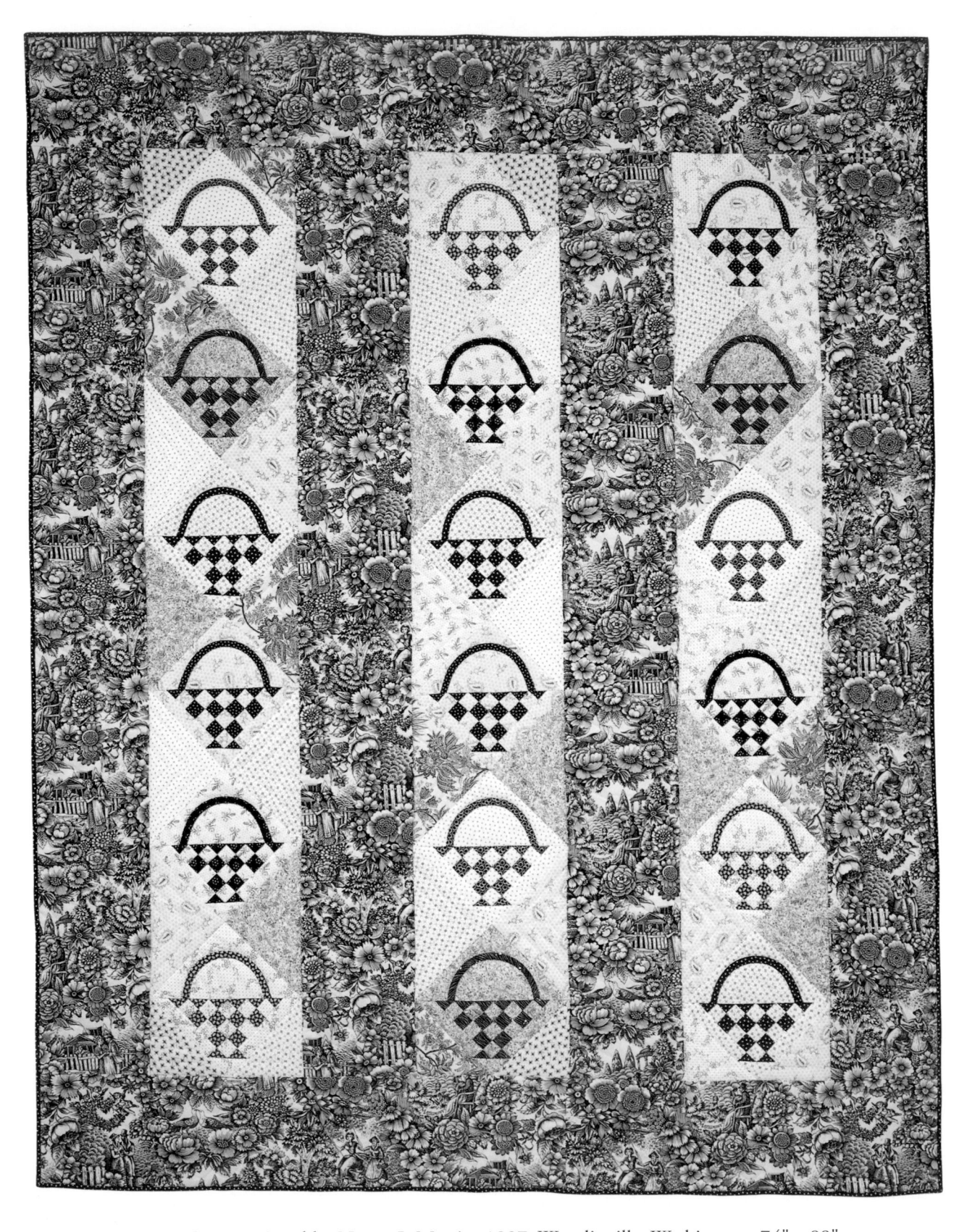

BASKET STACK, pieced by Nancy J. Martin, 1997, Woodinville, Washington, 74" x 88".
Basket blocks stitched in reproduction indigo fabrics are set strippy style.
A toile fabric used between the blocks and in the borders provides a pleasing contrast in scale.
Quilted by Mrs. Jr. E. Troyer.

3. Join light squares and dark triangles to the segments as shown to make the middle and lower rows, reversing the light and dark pieces from row to row.

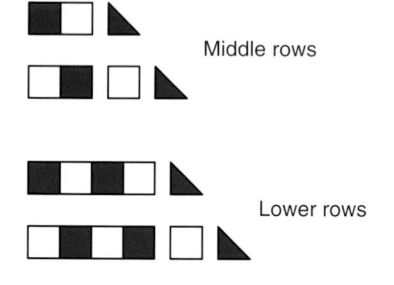

Middle rows

Lower rows

4. Add 2 dark triangles to 1 light square to make the upper row. Join the rows to form the basket.

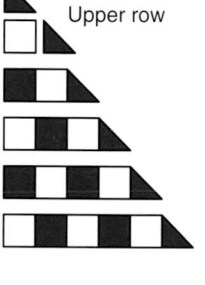

Upper row

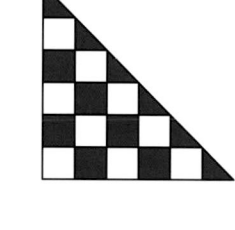

5. Join a dark triangle to a Basket Stack template piece and a template piece reversed. Add the units to the basket. Add a small light-background triangle to the lower corner of the basket.

6. Prepare the bias strips for the basket handles, following the directions on page 64. Using the placement template, arrange and appliqué the handles to the large light-background triangles.

7. Join a large background triangle to a basket unit to make 1 Basket block. Make 18 blocks.

8. Join 6 Basket blocks, 10 side setting triangles, and 4 corner setting triangles to make a vertical row. Make 3 rows.

9. Join the rows, placing vertical sashing between the rows and adding the side borders. Add the top and bottom borders.

10. Layer the quilt top with batting and backing. Tie or quilt. See the quilting suggestion below.

11. Bind the edges with the bias strips.

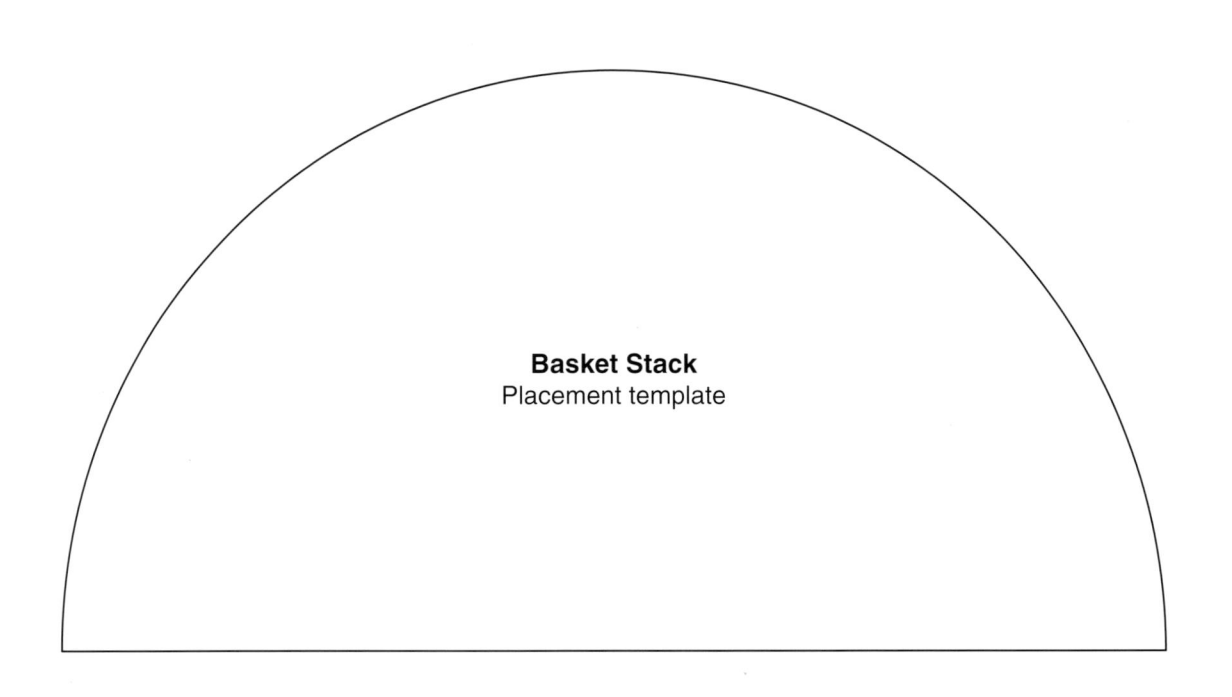

Basket Stack
Placement template

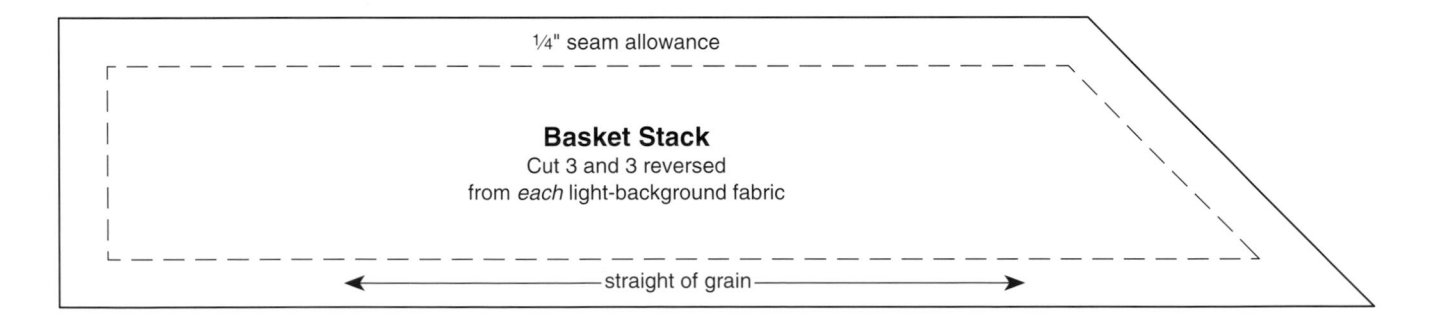

¼" seam allowance

Basket Stack
Cut 3 and 3 reversed
from *each* light-background fabric

←————————————— straight of grain —————————————→

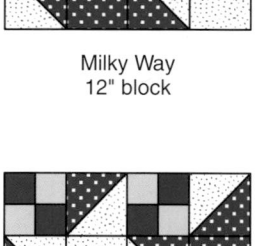

Milky Way
12" block

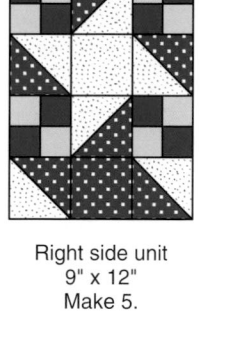

Right side unit
9" x 12"
Make 5.

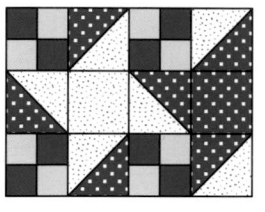

Bottom unit
9" x 12"
Make 5.

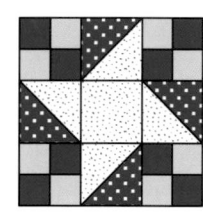

Corner unit
9" x 9"
Make 1 for lower right.

DIMENSIONS: 69" x 69"
FINISHED BLOCK SIZE: 12" x 12"

25 blocks, set 5 across and 5 down, with side, bottom, and corner units.

MATERIALS: 44"-WIDE FABRIC

9 fat quarters of navy blue prints with light background

9 fat quarters of navy blue prints with dark background

1 yd. dark navy blue fabric for four-patch units

1 yd. light blue fabric for four-patch units

4¼ yds. fabric for backing

⅝ yd. fabric for 284" (7⅞ yds.) of bias binding

CUTTING
ALL MEASUREMENTS INCLUDE ¼"-WIDE SEAMS.

From the fat quarters of navy blue prints with LIGHT background, cut a total of:

61 squares, each 3½" x 3½".

132 squares, each 3⅞" x 3⅞". Cut once diagonally to make 264 triangles.

From the fat quarters of navy blue prints with DARK background, cut a total of:

60 squares, each 3½" x 3½".

132 squares, each 3⅞" x 3⅞". Cut once diagonally to make 264 triangles.

From the dark navy blue fabric, cut:

30 strips, each 2" x 22", for four-patch units.

From the light blue fabric, cut:

30 strips, each 2" x 22", for four-patch units.

DIRECTIONS

1. Join the dark navy blue and light blue strips to make 30 strip sets. Press the seams toward the dark fabric. The strip sets should measure 3½" wide when sewn. Crosscut each strip set into 10 segments, each 2" wide, for a total of 300 units. You will use 288 units and have 12 left over.

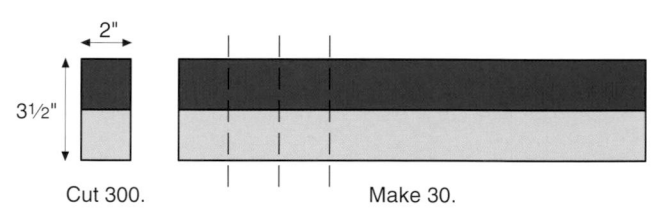

2"

3½"

Cut 300.   Make 30.

2. Join 2 segments as shown to make a four-patch unit. Make 144 units.

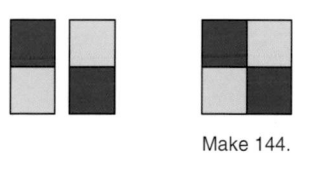

Make 144.

88

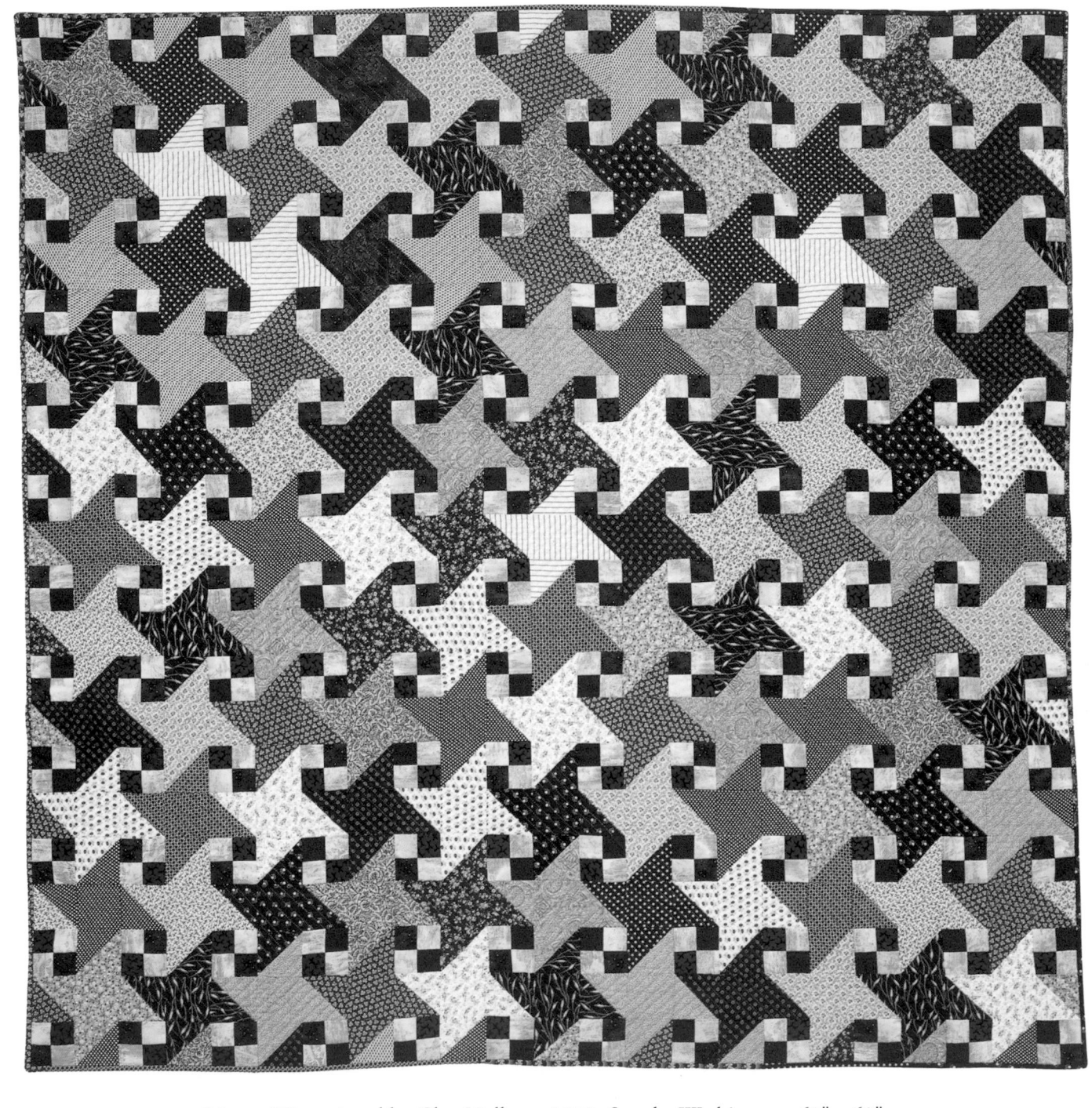

MILKY WAY, pieced by Cleo Nollette, 1992, Seattle, Washington, 69" x 69".
Indigo and light-background prints, longtime favorites with traditional quiltmakers, combine in this lively scrap quilt.
Quilted by Hazel Montague.

3. Join a navy blue triangle with dark background and a navy blue triangle with light background to make a half-square triangle unit. Make 264 triangle units.

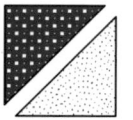 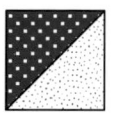

Make 264.

NOTE

Before you stitch the blocks, side, bottom, and corner units, arrange the elements on your design wall, taking care to match the fabrics in adjoining blocks and units. Use the quilt photo as a guide.

---

4. Arrange the four-patch units, triangle units, and 3½" squares into a block. Join the units into rows; press the seams in opposite directions from row to row. Join the rows to complete 1 Milky Way block. Make 25 blocks.

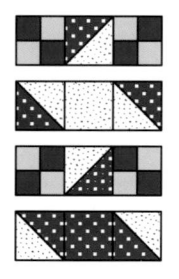

5. Join the blocks into 5 rows of 5 blocks each; press the seams in opposite directions from row to row. Join the rows; press the seams in the same direction.

6. Stitch 5 right side units; join the units. Press the seams in the opposite direction of the rows. Add the units to the right side of the quilt.

7. Stitch 5 bottom units; join the corner unit to the right end the opposite directi the units to th

8. g. Tie

Northern Nites

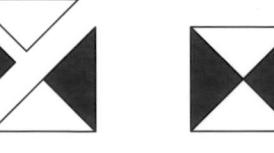

Old Favorite

DIMENSIONS: 60" x 76"

NOTE
This quilt is constructed in units as a bar quilt.
The units are joined into rows rather than blocks.

12 units, set 3 across and 4 down; 6"-wide border.

MATERIALS: 44"-WIDE FABRIC

2½ yds. white print for blocks
3¼ yds. dark blue print for blocks and border
3⅝ yds. fabric for backing (crosswise join)
⅝ yd. fabric for 280" (7¾ yds.) of bias binding

CUTTING
ALL MEASUREMENTS INCLUDE ¼"-WIDE SEAMS.

NOTE
Keep the half- and quarter-square triangles separate
to avoid confusion.

From the white print, cut:
13 strips, each 4½" x 42". Cut 2 of the strips into 28
    rectangles, each 2½" x 4½". Cut the remaining
    strips into 82 squares, each 4½" x 4½".
5 strips, each 2⅞" x 42". Cut the strips into 62
    squares, each 2⅞" x 2⅞". Cut once diagonally to
    make 124 half-square triangles.
2 strips, each 5¼" x 42". Cut the strips into 9
    squares, each 5¼" x 5¼". Cut twice diagonally
    to make 36 quarter-square triangles. You will use
    34 and have 2 left over.

From the dark blue print, cut:
3 strips, each 4⅞" x 42". Cut the strips into 24
    squares, each 4⅞" x 4⅞". Cut once diagonally to
    make 48 half-square triangles.
3 strips, each 4½" x 42". Cut the strips into 18
    squares, each 4½" x 4½", and 10 rectangles,
    each 2½" x 4½".

From the length of the remaining dark blue print, cut:
2 strips, each 2½" x 84". Cut into 52 squares, each
    2½" x 2½".
1 strip, 5¼" x 84". Cut the strip into 12 squares,
    each 5¼" x 5¼". Cut twice diagonally to make
    48 quarter-square triangles.
4 strips, each 7" x 84", for borders.

DIRECTIONS

1. Using 14 blue quarter-square triangles and 28
   white half-square triangles, piece 14 of Unit A.

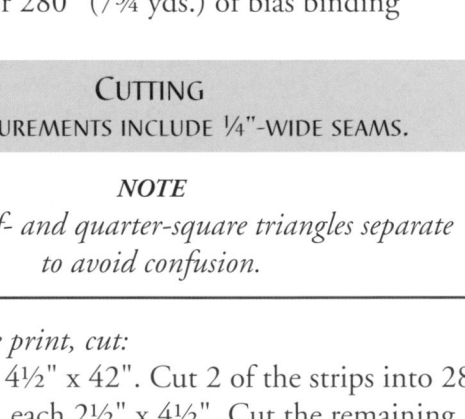

Unit A
Make 14.

2. Using 96 white half-square triangles, 48 blue
   2½" squares, and 48 blue half-square triangles,
   piece 48 of Unit B.

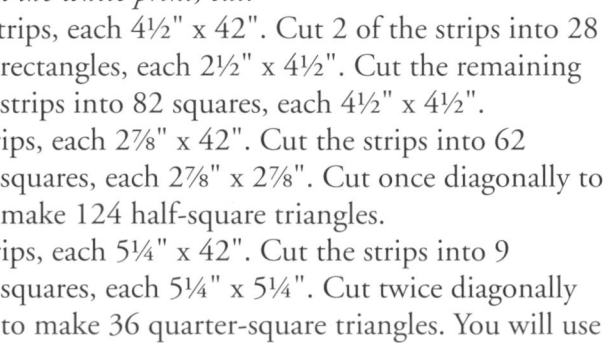

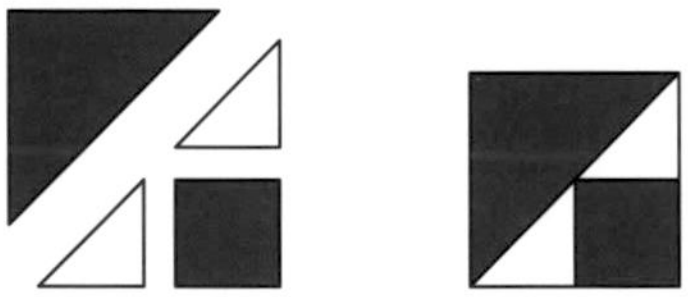

Unit B
Make 48.

3. Using the remaining 34 blue quarter-square
   triangles and 34 white quarter-square triangles,
   piece 17 of Unit C.

Unit C
Make 17.

91

4. Using 2 blue 2½" squares, 2 blue rectangles, 5 white rectangles, and 3 of Unit A, make Row A. Make an additional Row A.

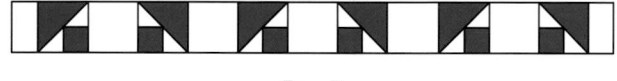

Row A
Make 2.

5. Using 5 white 4½" squares, 2 white rectangles, and 6 of Unit B, make Row B. Make 8 total of Row B.

Row B
Make 8.

6. Using 5 white 4½" squares, 3 blue 4½" squares, 2 of Unit A, and 2 of Unit C, make Row C. Make 4 total of Row C.

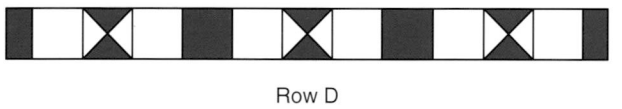

Row C
Make 4.

7. Using 5 white 4½" squares, 2 blue 4½" squares, 2 blue rectangles, and 3 of Unit C, make Row D. Make 3 total of Row D.

Row D
Make 3.

8. Join the rows as shown; rows marked * are turned upside down.

9. Add the borders, following the directions on pages 66–67.
10. Layer the quilt top with batting and backing. Tie or quilt. See the quilting suggestion below.
11. Bind the edges with the bias strips.

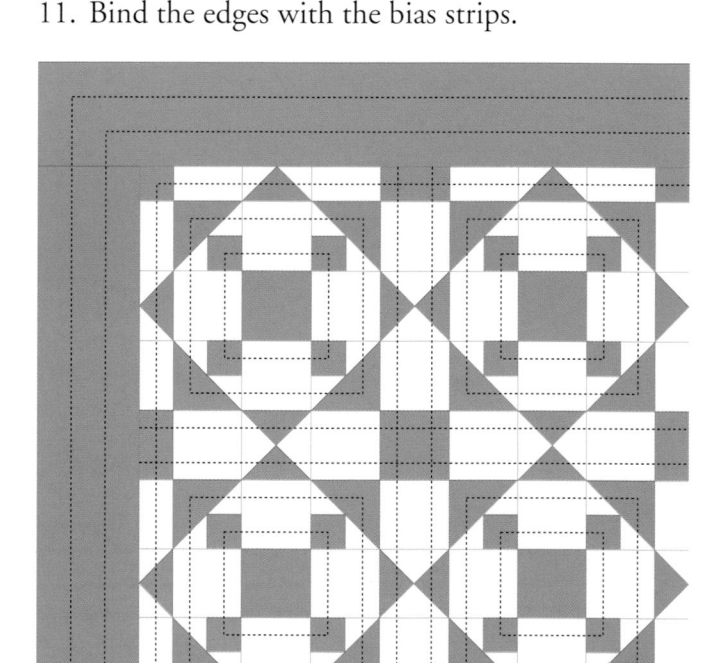

NORTHERN NITES, by Peggy Hinchey, 1991, Anchorage, Alaska, 60" x 76".
This graphic two-fabric quilt features blue and white prints in traditional Old Favorite blocks.

La Fête

DIMENSIONS: 36" x 32"

14" x 18" center medallion with 4 borders: 1"-wide checked border, 2"-wide Sawtooth border, 2"-wide print border, and 4"-wide pieced-triangle border.

MATERIALS: 44"-WIDE FABRIC

14½" x 18½" panel for medallion center*
¼ yd. checked fabric for inner border
⅜ yd. print fabric for print border
8 fat quarters of assorted light- and dark-background prints for Sawtooth border and pieced-triangle border
1 yd. fabric for backing
⅜ yd. fabric for 144" (4 yds.) of bias binding

* Center the design carefully when you cut the panel.

CUTTING
ALL MEASUREMENTS INCLUDE ¼"-WIDE SEAMS.

From the checked fabric, cut:
2 strips, each 1½" x 18½", for top and bottom inner borders.
2 strips, each 1½" x 16½", for side inner borders.

From the print fabric, cut:
4 strips, each 2½" x 24½", for top, bottom, and side borders.

From the assorted prints, cut:
10 squares, each 8" x 8", for bias squares. (You will need to cut 2 squares from 2 of the fabrics.) Pair the light- and dark-background squares; then cut and piece 2½"-wide bias strips, following the directions for bias squares on pages 57–59. Cut 8 bias squares, each 2½" x 2½", from each combination, for a total of 40 bias squares.

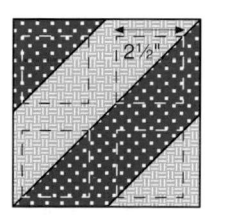

From the assorted prints and remaining border fabrics, cut:
30 squares, each 5¼" x 5¼". Cut twice diagonally to make 120 triangles for the pieced-triangle border.

DIRECTIONS

1. Stitch the 1½" x 18½" checked strips to the top and bottom of the panel. Stitch the 1½" x 16½" checked strips to the sides.

2. Join bias squares to make 2 border strips as shown, each with 10 bias squares. Stitch the strips to the long sides (top and bottom) of the center panel.

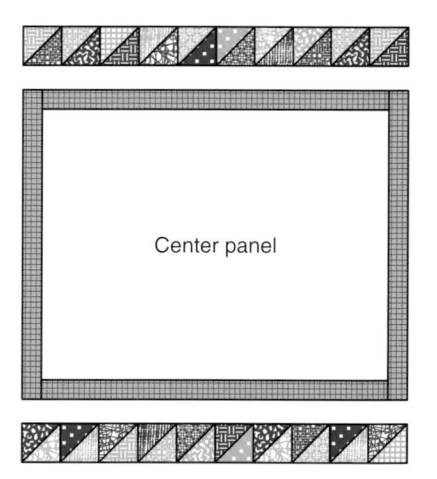

3. Join bias squares to make 2 border strips as shown, each with 10 bias squares. Stitch the strips to the short sides of the center panel. Note that dark pieces touch in the upper right and lower left corners.

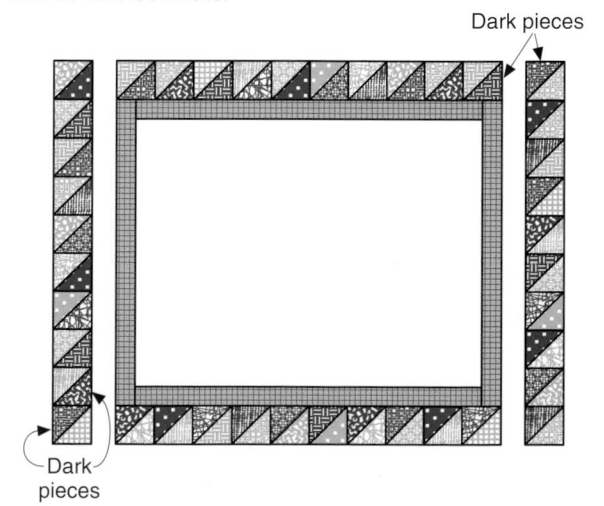

LA FÊTE, pieced by Nancy J. Martin, 1997, Woodinville, Washington, 36" x 32".
A toile fabric depicting a French festival in a country setting becomes the focus of this medallion-style wall hanging.
Sawtooth and triangle borders frame the center panel. Quilted by Alvina Nelson.

4. Stitch the 2½" x 24½" print strips to the top and bottom of the panel. Stitch the remaining strips to the sides.

5. Piece the triangle units as shown, mixing prints in each unit.

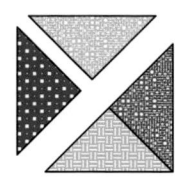

Make 30.

6. Piece 2 border strips with 6 triangle units each and 2 border strips with 9 triangle units each.

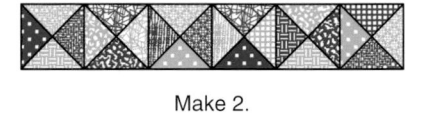

Make 2.

Make 2.

7. Stitch the short border strips to the sides of the quilt top. Stitch the long border strips to the top and bottom of the quilt top.

8. Layer the quilt top with batting and backing. Tie or quilt. See the quilting suggestion below.

9. Bind the edges with the bias strips.

Chinese Puzzle

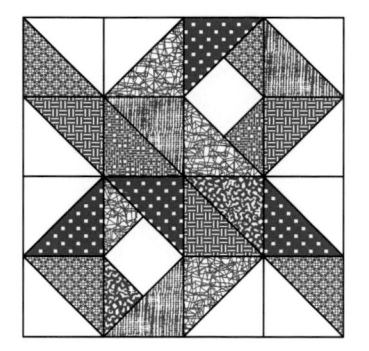

Chinese Puzzle

DIMENSIONS: 31¼" x 43"
FINISHED BLOCK SIZE: 10" x 10"

6 blocks, set 2 across and 3 down, with 1¾"-wide sashing and sashing squares; 3"-wide border.

MATERIALS: 44"-WIDE FABRIC

6 fat quarters of assorted light-background fabrics
6 fat quarters of assorted navy blue prints
½ yd. navy blue print for border
1⅜ yds. fabric for backing
⅜ yd. fabric for 158" (4½ yds.) of bias binding

CUTTING
ALL MEASUREMENTS INCLUDE ¼"-WIDE SEAMS.

From EACH fat quarter of light-background fabric, cut:
1 square (6 total), 12" x 12", for bias squares.
2 squares (12 total), each 2¼" x 2¼", for Piece B.
3 strips (18 total), each 2¼" x 10½", for sashing strips.

From EACH fat quarter of navy blue prints, cut:
1 square (6 total), 12" x 12", for bias squares. Pair each square with a 12" square of light-background fabric; then cut and piece 2¾"-wide bias strips, following the directions for bias squares on pages 57–59. Cut 60 bias squares, each 3" x 3".
4 squares (24 total), each 3⅜" x 3⅜". Cut once diagonally to make 48 half-square triangles for Piece A.

1 square (6 total), 3¾" x 3¾". Cut twice diagonally to make 24 quarter-square triangles for Piece C.
2 squares (12 total), each 2¼" x 2¼", for sashing squares.

From the navy blue print for the border, cut:
4 strips, each 3¼" x 43½". If your fabric is less than 44" wide after preshrinking, you will need to cut an additional strip and piece the border.

DIRECTIONS

1. Join a 2¼" light-background square (Piece B), 2 small navy blue triangles (Piece C), and 2 large navy blue triangles (Piece A) to make Unit 1. Make 12 units.

   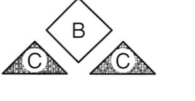

Unit 1
Make 12.

2. Join 2 navy blue triangles (Piece A) to make a navy blue/navy blue bias square. Make 12.

Make 12.

3. Join 1 navy blue/navy blue bias square, 5 light-background/navy blue bias squares, and Unit 1 to make a section. Make an additional section.

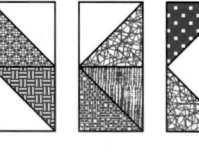 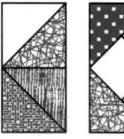  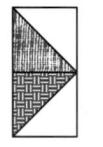

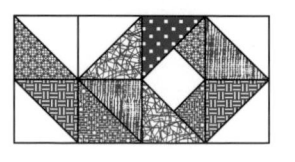

Make 2.

4. Join the sections, reversing the lower one, to make 1 Chinese Puzzle block. Make 6 blocks.

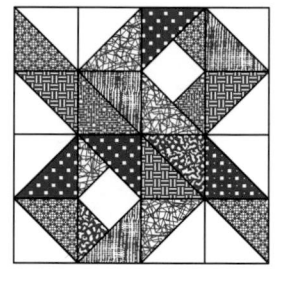

Make 6.

5. Join 2 blocks and 3 sashing strips to make a row. Make 3 rows.

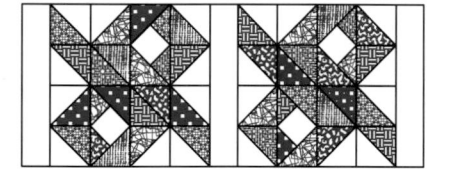

Make 3.

6. Join 2 sashing strips and 3 sashing squares to make a sashing row. Make 4 sashing rows.

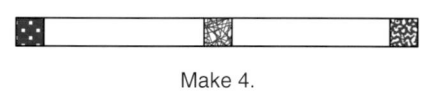

Make 4.

7. Join the rows of blocks and sashing strips as shown in the quilt photo.
8. Add the navy blue border, following the directions for borders on pages 66–67.
9. Layer the quilt top with batting and backing. Tie or quilt. See the quilting suggestion below.
10. Bind the edges with the bias strips.

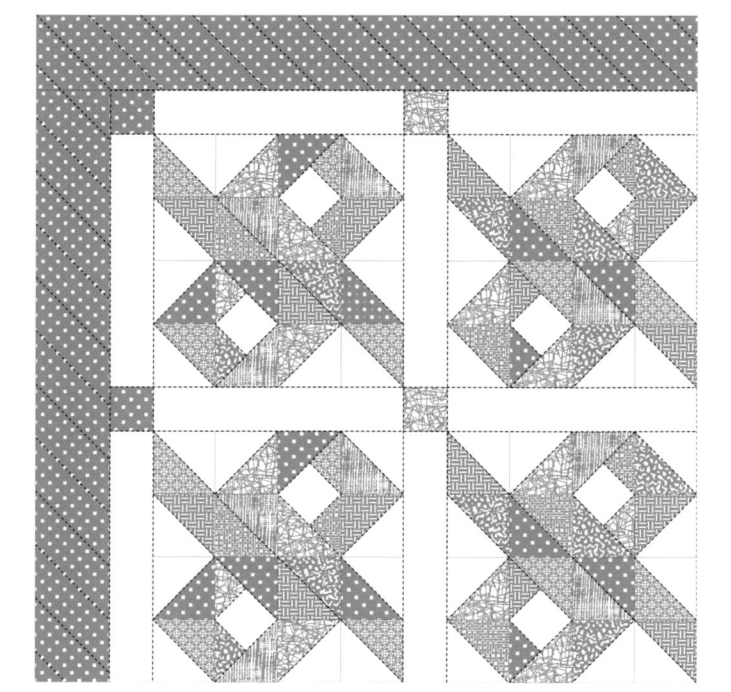

CHINESE PUZZLE, pieced by Nancy J. Martin, 1992, Woodinville, Washington, 31¼" x 43".
Japanese kimono fabrics collected on a trip to Australia make this Chinese Puzzle pattern a true international quilt.
The dark blue fabrics represent the two interlocking loops in this age-old mind teaser. Quilted by Roxanne Carter.

Darting Minnows

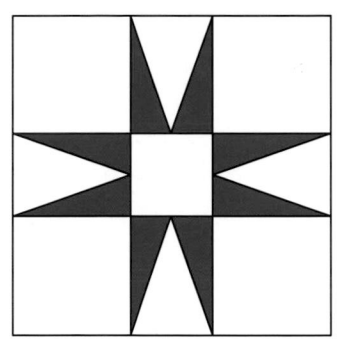

Darting Minnows

DIMENSIONS: 77½" x 104½"

NOTE
To eliminate unnecessary seams, this quilt is constructed in units as a bar quilt. The units are joined into rows rather than blocks.

3½", 5", and 10" units joined in 2 bar formats; 5"-wide border.

MATERIALS: 44"-WIDE FABRIC

7 yds. white fabric for background and borders
2⅞ yds. navy blue fabric for minnows
6¼ yds. fabric for backing (crosswise join)
¾ yd. fabric for 372" (10⅓ yds.) of bias binding

CUTTING
ALL MEASUREMENTS INCLUDE ¼"-WIDE SEAMS.

From the white fabric, cut:
2 strips, each 5¼" x 95", along the lengthwise grain, for side borders.
2 strips, each 5¼" x 77½", along the lengthwise grain, for top and bottom borders.
24 squares, each 10½" x 10½".
35 squares, each 4" x 4".
20 rectangles, each 5½" x 10½", for outer edges.
4 squares, each 5½" x 5½", for corners.
58 Template 1.
24 Template 2.

From the navy blue fabric, cut:
140 Template 3.
140 Template 3 reversed.

DIRECTIONS

1. Piece 58 minnow units using Pieces 1, 3, and 3 reversed. Each pieced unit should measure 4" x 10½" when sewn.

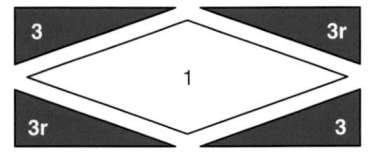

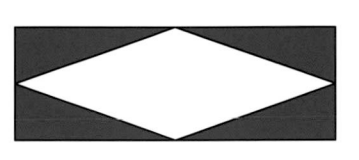

Make 58.

2. Piece 24 outer-edge minnow units, using pieces 2, 3, and 3 reversed. Each unit should measure 4" x 5½" when sewn.

Make 24.

3. Join 4 minnow units, five 4" squares, and 2 outer-edge minnow units to make 1 bar. Make 7 bars.

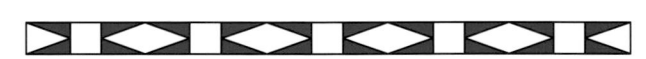

Make 7.

4. Join 5 minnow units, four 10½" squares, and two 5½" x 10½" rectangles to make 1 bar. Make 6 bars.

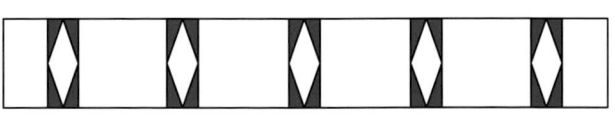

Make 6.

DARTING MINNOWS, pieced by Cleo Nollette, 1997, Seattle, Washington, 77½" x 104½".
Crisp navy blue and white fabrics create a bold design, with plenty of space for hand quilting.
Quilted by Mrs. Sam Swartzentruber.

5. Join two 5½" corner squares, 5 outer-edge minnow units, and four 5½" x 10½" rectangles to make 1 bar for the top edge. Make an additional bar for the bottom edge.

Make 1 for top.
Make 1 for bottom.

6. Arrange the bars as shown, alternating the wide and narrow bars. Join the bars.

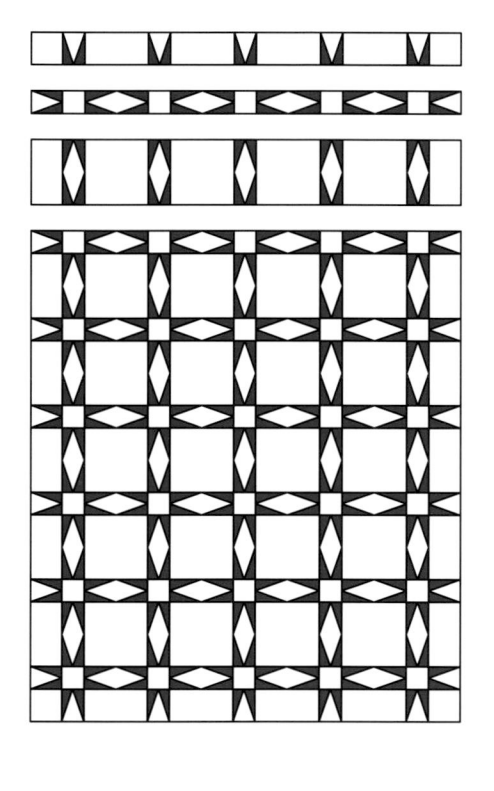

7. Add the side borders, following the directions for borders on pages 66–67. Add the top and bottom borders.
8. Layer the quilt top with batting and backing. Tie or quilt. See the quilting suggestion below.
9. Bind the edges with the bias strips.

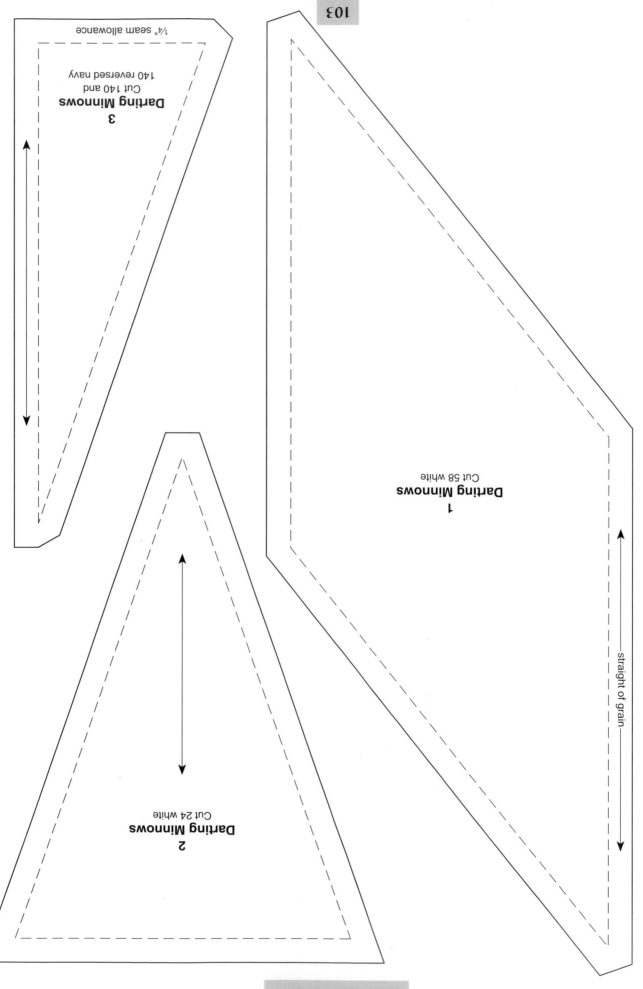

DARTING MINNOWS

¹⁄₄" seam allowance

Darting Minnows
3
Cut 140 and
140 reversed navy

Darting Minnows
1
Cut 58 white

straight of grain

Darting Minnows
2
Cut 24 white

Hens and Chicks

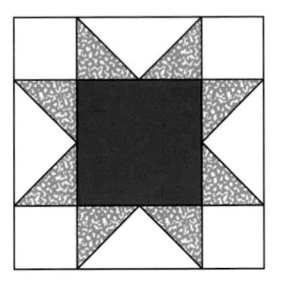

Hens and Chicks

Sawtooth Star

DIMENSIONS: 54" X 66"
FINISHED BLOCK SIZE: 10" X 10"

12 blocks, set 3 across and 4 down, with 2"-wide sashing and sashing squares; random 10" pieced border with six 8" Sawtooth Star blocks (3 blocks in opposite corners).

MATERIALS: 44"-WIDE FABRIC

⅞ yd. each of 6 light-background fabrics
6 fat quarters of dark-background fabrics
3¼ yds. fabric for backing (crosswise join)
½ yd. fabric for 248" (6⅞ yds.) of bias binding

CUTTING
ALL MEASUREMENTS INCLUDE ¼"-WIDE SEAMS.

From EACH light-background fabric, cut:
1 square (6 total), 8" x 8", for bias squares.
8 rectangles (48 total), each 2½" x 4½", for blocks.
8 squares (48 total), each 2⅞" x 2⅞". Cut once diagonally to make 96 small triangles for Hens and Chicks blocks.
3 strips (18 total), each 2½" x 10½", for sashing. You will use 17 and have 1 left over.
1 square (6 total), 2½" x 2½", for sashing squares.

From the remaining light-background fabrics, cut the following pieces randomly for the total amounts indicated:
2½"-wide strips in varying lengths for pieced border.
26 squares, each 6½" x 6½", for pieced border.
24 squares, each 2½" x 2½", for Sawtooth Star corners.
2 squares, each 4½" x 4½", for Sawtooth Star centers.
6 squares, each 5¼" x 5¼". Cut twice diagonally to make 24 large triangles for Sawtooth Stars.

From EACH fat quarter of dark-background fabric, cut:
1 square (6 total), 8" x 8", for bias squares. Pair each square with an 8" square of light-background fabric; then cut and piece 2½"-wide bias strips, following the directions for bias squares on pages 57–59. Cut a total of 48 bias squares, each 2½" x 2½", for Hens and Chicks blocks.

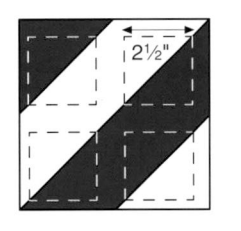

2 squares (12 total), each 2½" x 2½", for Hens and Chicks block centers.
4 squares (24 total), each 4⅞" x 4⅞". Cut once diagonally to make 48 large triangles for Hens and Chicks blocks.

From the remaining dark fat quarters, cut the following pieces randomly for the total amounts indicated:
24 squares, each 2⅞" x 2⅞". Cut once diagonally to make 48 small triangles for Sawtooth Star points.
4 squares, each 4½" x 4½", for Sawtooth Star centers.

HENS AND CHICKS, pieced by Nancy J. Martin, 1996, Woodinville, Washington, 54" x 66".
Soft background prints play a supporting role in this scrappy quilt. A random pieced border, accented by Sawtooth Stars in opposite corners, adds to the whimsical mood. Quilted by Mrs. Henry Schlabach.

DIRECTIONS

NOTE
Use matching light and dark fabrics for each block.

1. Join 2 bias squares, 4 small light triangles, 2 large dark triangles, and 1 light 2½" x 4½" rectangle. Make an additional unit.

  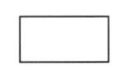 

Make 2.

2. Join 2 light 2½" x 4½" rectangles and 1 dark 2½" center square.

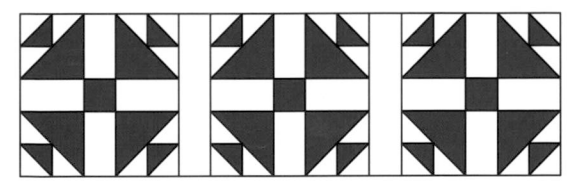

Make 1.

3. Join the units made in Steps 1 and 2 to make 1 Hens and Chicks block. Make 12 blocks.

Make 12.

4. Join 3 blocks and 2 sashing strips to make a row. Make 4 rows.

   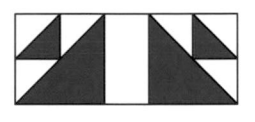

Make 4.

5. Join 3 sashing strips and 2 sashing squares to make a sashing row. Make 3 sashing rows.

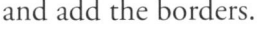

Make 3.

6. Join the rows, alternating rows of blocks and sashing.

7. Join 4 large light triangles, 8 small dark triangles, 4 light squares, and 1 dark 4½" center square to make 1 Sawtooth Star block. Make a total of 6 blocks, but leave the lower seam of one block unstitched; it will be joined when you assemble and add the borders.

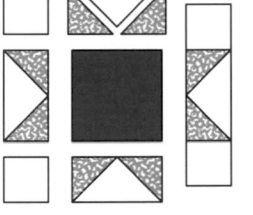 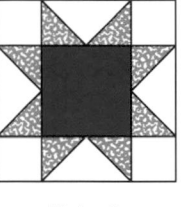

Make 6.

8. Randomly piece light 2½"-wide strips, 6½" squares, and 1 Sawtooth Star block for the left border. Add the border to the left side of the quilt top.

NOTE
Mix and match the strips so each border features a different combination of light fabrics.

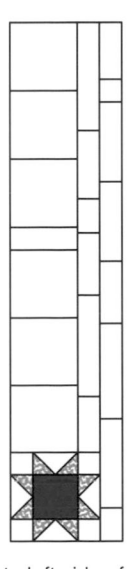

Join to left side of quilt.

9. Randomly piece 2½"-wide strips, 6½" squares, the lower section of the Sawtooth Star block, and a complete Sawtooth Star block for the right border. Add the border to the right side of the quilt top.

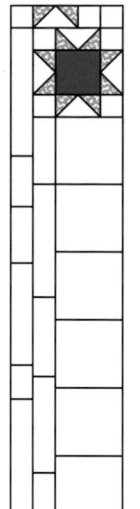

Join to right side of quilt.

10. Randomly piece 2½"-wide strips, 6½" squares, the upper section of the Sawtooth Star block, and a complete Sawtooth Star block for the top border. Add the border to the top of the quilt top.

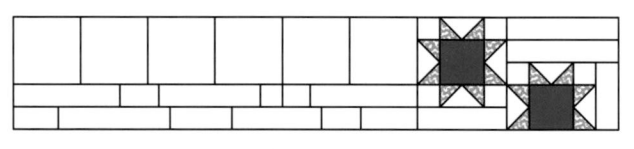

Join to top of quilt.

11. Randomly piece 2½"-wide strips, 6½" squares, and 2 Sawtooth Star blocks for the bottom border. Add the border to the bottom of the quilt top.

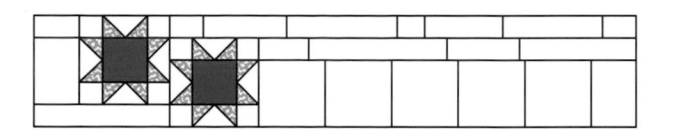

Join to bottom of quilt.

12. Layer the quilt top with batting and backing. Tie or quilt. See the quilting suggestion below.
13. Bind the edges with the bias strips.

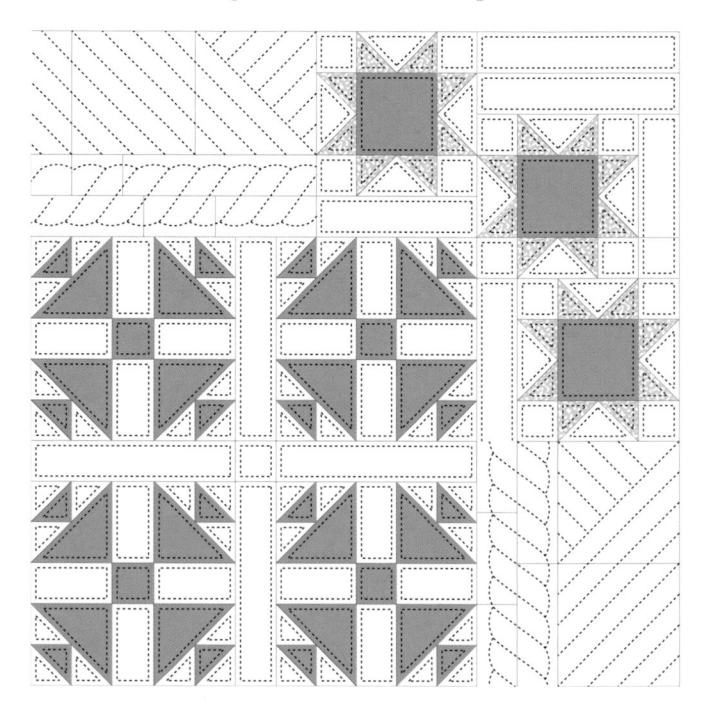

Union Square

Union Square

DIMENSIONS: 74¼" X 91¼"
FINISHED BLOCK SIZE: 12" X 12"

12 blocks, set diagonally with alternate plain blocks and side and corner setting triangles; 1½"-wide inner border, 4¼"-wide pieced ribbon middle border, and 6"-wide outer border.

MATERIALS: 44"-WIDE FABRIC

5 yds. white tone-on-tone fabric for background and borders
½ yd. light blue print for star centers and squares
½ yd. dark blue print #1 for star points
⅝ yd. blue checked fabric for stars and ribbon border
1⅜ yds. dark blue print #2 for bias squares and ribbon border
4¾ yds. fabric for backing (crosswise join)
¾ yd. fabric for 344" (9½ yds.) of bias binding

CUTTING
ALL MEASUREMENTS INCLUDE ¼"-WIDE SEAMS.

From the white tone-on-tone fabric, cut:
4 strips, each 6¼" x 82", along the lengthwise grain, for outer border.
4 strips, each 2" x 68½", along the lengthwise grain, for inner border.
12 squares, each 5¼" x 5¼". Cut twice diagonally to make 48 triangles for blocks.

48 squares, each 2½" x 2½", for blocks.
3 fat quarters, each 18" x 22", for bias squares.
3 squares, each 18¼" x 18¼". Cut twice diagonally to make 12 side setting triangles. You will use 10 and have 2 left over.
2 squares, each 9½" x 9½". Cut once diagonally to make 4 corner setting triangles.
2 squares, each 6¾" x 6¾". Cut once diagonally to make 4 triangles for corners of ribbon border.
12 squares, each 4⅛" x 4⅛". Cut twice diagonally to make 48 small triangles for ribbon border. You will use 46 and have 2 left over.
11 squares, each 7" x 7". Cut twice diagonally to make 44 large triangles for ribbon border. You will use 42 and have 2 left over.

From the light blue print, cut:
12 squares, each 4½" x 4½", for block centers.
48 squares, each 2½" x 2½", for blocks.

From the dark blue print #1, cut:
24 squares, each 5¼" x 5¼". Cut twice diagonally to make 96 triangles for star points.

From the blue checked fabric, cut:
12 squares, each 5¼" x 5¼". Cut twice diagonally to make 48 triangles for blocks.
46 squares, each 2½" x 2½", for ribbon border.

From the dark blue print #2, cut:
46 squares, each 2½" x 2½", for ribbon border.
11 squares, each 4⅛" x 4⅛". Cut twice diagonally to make 44 small triangles for ribbon border. You will use 42 and have 2 left over.
3 fat quarters, each 18" x 22", for bias squares. Pair each blue fat quarter with a white fat quarter; then cut and piece 2½"-wide bias strips, following the directions for bias squares on pages 57–59. Cut 142 bias squares, each 2½" x 2½".

UNION SQUARE, pieced by Nancy J. Martin, 1997, Woodinville, Washington, 74¼" x 91¼".
A white tone-on-tone fabric in the alternate blocks and wide borders allows plenty of room for elaborate quilting.
A pieced ribbon border frames the on-point blocks. Quilted by Alvina Nelson.

DIRECTIONS

1. Piece 48 of Unit 1, using 2½" bias squares, light print squares, and white background squares.

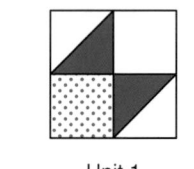

Unit 1
Make 48.

2. Piece 48 of Unit 2, using dark blue print #1, checked, and white background triangles.

Unit 2
Make 48.

3. Join two of Unit 1 and a Unit 2. Make 2 sections. Join two of Unit 2 and a center square. Join the sections to make 1 Union Square block. Make 12 blocks.

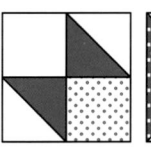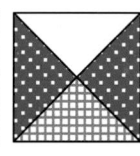

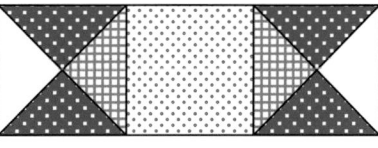

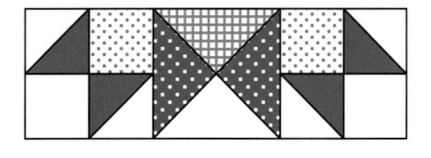

Make 12.

4. Arrange and join Union Square blocks, alternate blocks, and side setting triangles into diagonal rows. Press the seam allowances away from the pieced blocks. Join the diagonal rows; add the corner setting triangles.

5. Add the 2"-wide white inner border strips to the quilt top, following the directions for borders on pages 66–67. After adding the inner borders, the quilt top should measure 54¼" x 71¼", including seam allowances. Adjust the inner border width to match these dimensions.

6. Arrange and piece bias squares, dark blue print #2 squares and triangles, checked squares, and small and large white triangles as shown to make 2 borders for the sides.

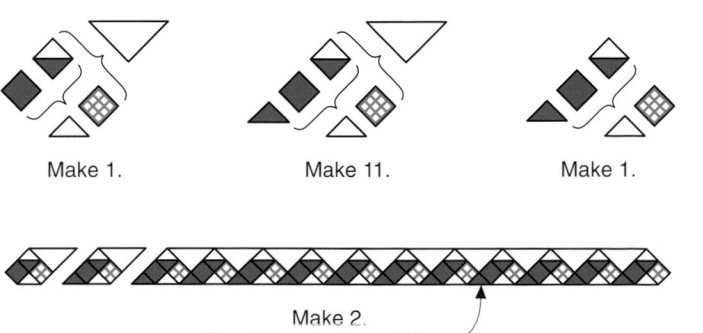

Make 1.   Make 11.   Make 1.

Make 2.
Sew this edge to quilt top.

7. Piece 2 borders as shown for the top and bottom.

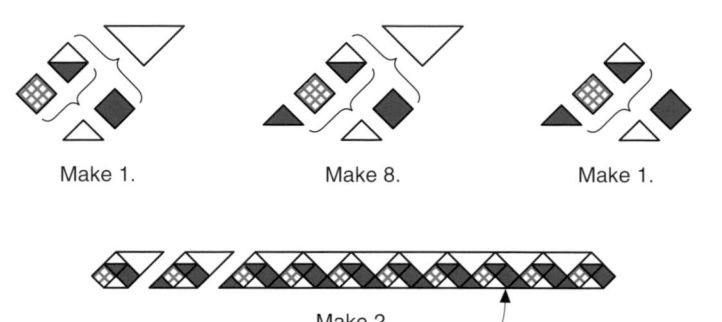

Make 1.   Make 8.   Make 1.

Make 2.
Sew this edge to quilt top.

8. Stitch the borders to the sides and top and bottom of the quilt, matching corner-square colors. Begin and end the stitching ¼" from the corners of the quilt, leaving the seam at the corner open.

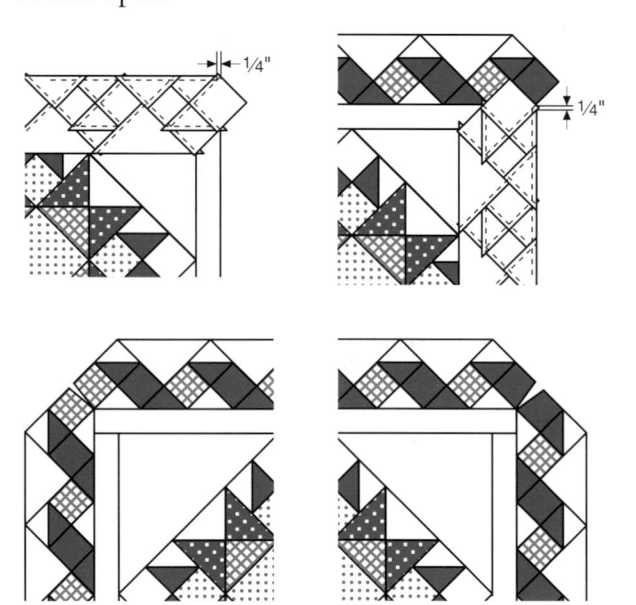

¼"

¼"

9. Stitch the borders together at each corner.

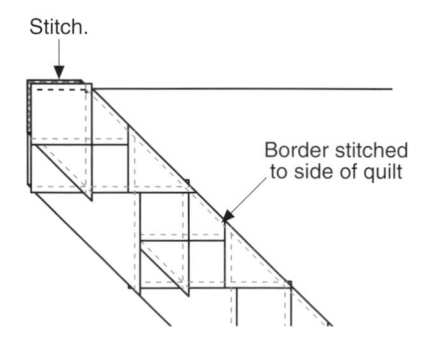

Stitch.

Border stitched to side of quilt

10. Add the white triangles to the corners of the borders, trimming the excess if needed.

11. Add the 6¼"-wide white outer borders, following the directions for borders on pages 66–67.
12. Layer the quilt top with batting and backing. Tie or quilt. See the quilting suggestion below.
13. Bind the edges with the bias strips.